American Dream, American Burnout

How to Cope When It All Gets to Be Too Much

Also by Gerald Loren Fishkin, Ph.D.

Police Burnout
Signs, Symptoms and Solutions

and

Firefighter and Paramedic Burnout
The Survival Guide — The Role You Play

American Dream, American Burnout

How to Cope When It All Gets to Be Too Much

Gerald Loren Fishkin, Ph.D.

Library of Congress Catalog Card Number:
93-91727

ISBN: 0-9638371-0-9

Printed in the United States of America

First Edition
April 1994

*This book is dedicated
to the loving memory
of my Mother and Father.*

Contents

CHAPTER NINE
Working Through a Life Crisis 97

CHAPTER TEN
Burnout — A Modern American Epidemic 111

Foreword

*American Dream, American Burnout —
How to Cope When It All Gets to Be Too
Much* covers a vital mental health issue in
a way that is both scholarly and highly
readable.

In my 35 years of practicing Internal
Medicine, I have seen great changes in the
quality and character of my patients' lives.
Among the hundreds of cases I see every
year, burnout is a surprisingly common
thread. My observation has been that the
enthusiasm and idealism of the 1950s has
given way to apathy, fear and depression in
the '90s.

I firmly believe that a responsible physician should always evaluate the mind of
the patient, as well as his or her body. In
fact, the body and mind should be regarded

as one, or at least as two strongly intercon-
nected elements, both of which undeni-
ably influence one another.

As an internist/cardiologist, I see numerous patients with the complaints that
Dr. Fishkin writes about. In fact, since pre-
viewing the book, I have begun asking
them to take the Self-Test on pages xxv-
xxvi. Of course, I carefully investigate complaints such as insomnia, stomach pains,
palpitations, headaches, increased alcohol
usage, anxiety, depression and other disorders. But, often after ruling out physical
disease, a combination of the Self-Test and
a carefully taken history will lead me to a
diagnosis of burnout.

The first step in the treatment of burnout is acknowledging that you are suffering

from it. The second is finding help. In this pursuit, I believe that Dr. Fishkin has written the definitive book on overcoming burnout and its associated dysfunctions. As a person who has spent his life looking for solutions to problems, I particularly appreciated Chapter 11, "Solutions for Dealing with Burnout." I absolutely agree with the philosophy endorsed in the Postscript, as well.

Epictetus, a first century philosopher, said, "People are upset not by events, but by how they view them." Dr. Fishkin's methods for attitude restructuring show us how to overcome the negativity barrier and make a serious commitment to understanding ourselves and others. He reminds us to learn to recognize and identify the stressors in our lives, and to be aware of what is going on inside and outside ourselves.

Optimism, Dr. Fishkin reminds us, "should be used as a beacon." I would like to add to this the "Five Virtues" of enthusiasm, belief, love, forgiveness and perseverance. To those who want to lead a meaningful life, not just an existence, to those who want to be happy and healthy, I heartily recommend this landmark book.

Arnold Fox, M.D.
Author,
The Beverly Hills Medical Diet
Beverly Hills, California

Acknowledgments

FOR ME, THE MOST DIFFICULT PART of the closure of any project is to adequately express the depth of my thanks and appreciation to the many people involved. This book is no exception.

Offsetting a significant part of the uncertainty and anxiety inherent in projecting my ideas onto a blank page has been the opportunity to work with individuals of the highest personal and professional caliber. All of these individuals have made invaluable contributions to this book, and I wish to thank them individually and collectively.

First, my sincere gratitude to Eleanor S. Szanton, Ph.D., executive director of the National Center for Clinical Infant Programs at Arlington, Virginia, for providing research source material on developmental problems associated with infant and childhood stress. Further appreciation goes to Susan A. Uretzky, MPH, associate director of the March of Dimes Birth Defects Foundation, Burbank, California, for data related to maternal abuse on a national level, and Christine Baker, chief of the Department of Industrial Relations, Division of Labor Statistics and Research, San Francisco, California, for current data related to work-related, disabling, non-fatal stress and stress-related disorders and cases.

Many thanks also to Alexander W. Astin, Ph.D., professor and director of the Cooperative Institutional Research Program, and his staff at UCLA's Higher Education Research Institute, for providing me with ongoing data regarding the Annual National Report on College Freshman's Attitudes, Values and Life Goals, and Linda R. Washington, public affairs specialist at the U.S. Department of Health and Human Services, Public Health Service, Centers for Disease Control, Maryland, for providing me with the center's Monthly Report of Final Mortality Statistics, as well as its report on Births, Marriages, Divorces and Deaths, including data associated with causal factors.

Ralph Waldo Emerson once said that an author is never successful until he has learned to make his words smaller than his ideas. In that respect, I have been very fortunate to have had the editorial assistance of two individuals who have not only been a pleasure to work with but were able to clarify some of my more esoteric thoughts into a coherent and readable form. Clarence Henderson, my technical editor, has the consummate ability to summarize and integrate hundreds of pieces of data into a meaningful and cohesive whole, and Carol Carlsen Brooks, my text editor, kept my prose prosaic and insisted that I obey the rules of grammar and syntax.

Alan Leghart deserves special thanks, also, for his design and implementation of the final manuscript, as well as his creative contributions and computer wizardry throughout the entire project. Much essential help was also provided by Heidi Hatton, my secretary and confidant, whose extraordinary patience in coping with my sometimes madcap behavior and superlative skill in the handling of the manuscript made everyone's job a lot easier.

John Malmström applied his creativity and artistry to the design and production of the book's cover, and blessed me with his wise counsel and continuous support in overseeing every aspect of its production.

This book also owes a great debt to the advice and encouragement I received from my emotional support team. Irwin Zucker, president of Promotion in Motion, Hollywood, California, my friend and mentor in the world of public relations, is always there when I need him. Meyer Fisher, senior vice president, Harcourt Brace Jovanovich, Legal and Professional Publications, Inc., has been generous with his encouragement, support and belief in me and the value of this project from the outset.

I would also like to acknowledge John A. Ackerman, president of Fire Publications, for his contributions throughout the final production stages of this project.

At the heart of this support group is my wife Kathy, my true love, best friend and partner in life. Without her constant support, encouragement and understanding, this book would not have been possible.

Finally, I would like to thank all of my patients over the years, who have validated my belief that the most important necessities in life are balance, meaning and purpose. To them, my deepest gratitude. 📖

Introduction

"I'm tired all the time."
"I must be losing it."
"I just can't find a reason to get up in the morning any more."

THOUGHTS AND FEELINGS SUCH AS THESE may have caused you to pick up this book. Or maybe a loved one is experiencing these disturbing symptoms or is attempting to cope with them through drugs, alcohol or other compulsive behaviors.

Chances are, if you've expressed any of the above statements to a friend or co-worker, he or she told you, "Oh, you're just burned out. Take a vacation! Eat better and get more sleep. And for Heaven's sake, cheer up!"

Physical symptoms such as chronic fatigue, insomnia or digestive problems may drive you to a physician, only to be told in so many words that it's all in your head · — you don't react well to the stress in your life. Proffered solutions usually include tranquilizing drugs or advice to summarily "eliminate the stress from your life," as if you could simply find a new job, trade in

an unsupportive spouse or chuck it all to go live on a tropical island.

Well-meaning therapists who are unversed in the treatment of burnout may tell you your problems are caused by a "wounded inner child" or growing up in a dysfunctional family. This gives you someone or something to blame, but also serves to absolve you of the responsibility to take charge of your own life.

The only thing the experts and your own intuition agree on is that you are suffering from burnout, but just what is this elusive malady? First of all, some background. The term "Burn-Out" was first coined in the early 1960s to describe the state of physical and mental depletion observed among workers in alternative health care agencies (such as community mental health agencies, free clinics and volunteer counseling and family service agencies) whose jobs imposed detrimental work-related conditions like long hours, low pay and constantly dealing with crises.

In subsequent years, psychologists applied the term primarily to human service providers (like psychotherapists, social workers and counselors, both paid and volunteer) who exhibited symptoms such as emotional depletion, disillusionment, despair and despondency. More recently, "burnout" has been widely used to describe anything from on-the-job boredom to major depression. An unfortunate consequence of this loose usage of the term is that it has been trivialized, and the genuine sufferer is not well served by the folk wisdom that the cure for burnout is to take a vacation, get more sleep or simply "snap out of it."

As described in this book, burnout is a state of mental, emotional and physical exhaustion; its symptoms include cynicism, despair and demoralization. The most telling evidence that burnout exists is if you feel exhausted and depressed almost all the time, if there seems to be little meaning or purpose to your life, *and you are unable to continue to cope with the stressful events in your life.* (The latter distinction is important, because, while some forms of depression may arise without apparent cause in those whose lives are relatively orderly and calm, burnout can only affect you if you are subjected to stress, stress that you used to be able to handle, but that now seems overwhelming.)

Additionally, burnout often leads to unsuccessful coping mechanisms like substance abuse, excessive eating or spending and emotional withdrawal. Left to its ultimate conclusion, burnout leads to thoughts of suicide and death — anything to escape the meaningless, painful existence that life has become.

If you are suffering from burnout, you are not alone. While the diagnosis of burnout is often applied much too casually, it is by no means an unusual condition. Pick up any newspaper today, and you will be presented with ample evidence that we live in a stressful society. The economy is floundering, divorce is at an all-time high, children are growing up illiterate, senior citizens live out their remaining years in isolation and, often, financial straits and, we are told, there is a war going on between the sexes.

The wonder is not that burnout is widespread, but that it is not universal!

And yet, it is not. My experience as a psychotherapist dealing primarily with workers in high-stress occupations, as well as my research and writing on burnout among public safety personnel, has convinced me that neither the intensity nor the frequency of negative events or stressors on the job necessarily correlate to an increase in burnout. Every occupation involves some degree of stress. That's why it's called *work*. Otherwise, it would be called *play*, and you wouldn't get paid for it! Rather, it is the interaction of the occupation's negative aspects and the person's resources — or lack of resources — for dealing with them that leads to burnout. In other words, burnout requires both the susceptible personality and the stressful situation.

Can your burnout be alleviated? Absolutely! It is possible to lead a productive, more personally gratifying life, even in a stressful world. However, it requires a willingness to make fundamental life changes where necessary. These changes may or may not be external. Obviously, you may want or need to continue in your already defined occupational, social and/or family roles. Working through burnout in these circumstances means that the changes must come from within, particularly in the area of values and attitudes about life and work.

This book will give you a clearer understanding of the many causes of burnout, and help identify the stressors that trigger its symptoms within you. Finally, it will provide you with strategies to develop the skills to withstand life's stressors and crises *before* they occur.

Many of the anecdotal and case histories presented in this book were taken directly from my clinical files, and the identities of individuals profiled have been disguised.

Finally, I sincerely hope that this book will serve as a guide and an inspiration to the many sufferers of burnout. To you, I say, Take heart; there is a more satisfying, meaningful life ahead.

GERALD LOREN FISHKIN, PH.D.
Los Angeles, California

Self-Test
Are You Burned Out?

Symptoms

Check all boxes that apply

- ❑ I'm tired all the time, even after a full night's rest.
- ❑ I have trouble falling asleep, sleep restlessly or wake up much too early.
- ❑ It's getting harder and harder just to get up in the morning.
- ❑ I have a constant ache in my stomach and/or suffer from ulcers, gastritis or irritable/inflammatory colon.
- ❑ I get dizzy spells and heart palpitations or suffer pain that no doctor has been able to diagnose.
- ❑ I tend to overeat.
- ❑ I consume more alcohol than I should and/or rely on unprescribed drugs.
- ❑ Sometimes I go on shopping sprees and spend more than I can afford.
- ❑ I've been really accident-prone lately.
- ❑ I frequently burst into tears, and I don't know why.

Thoughts and Feelings

Check emotions you agree with or have felt recently.

- ❑ Life is basically meaningless.
- ❑ Every day is just like the next — what's the point?
- ❑ Almost no one understands or cares about me.
- ❑ Why won't everyone just leave me alone?
- ❑ No matter how hard I try, I always fail.
- ❑ I have to do everything myself; nobody will lend a hand.

- ❑ My co-workers are a bunch of idiots/are out to sabotage my job.
- ❑ I don't know how much longer I can continue to cope.
- ❑ Sometimes I just want to end it all.

Stressors

Check conditions that apply to you.

Work

- ❑ I don't get paid near enough for what I do.
- ❑ I'm qualified for a much better job.
- ❑ There's never enough time to finish all my work.
- ❑ My job involves solving crises on a regular basis.
- ❑ I could use a lot more assistance in doing my job.
- ❑ I've been missing a lot of work lately, and I'm always in trouble on the job.
- ❑ My job interferes with my personal life.
- ❑ My boss/co-workers are unsupportive/critical.
- ❑ I could lose my job at any time.

Personal

- ❑ I am recently divorced.
- ❑ My marriage is in trouble.
- ❑ I am raising children as a single parent.
- ❑ I am a caregiver for someone who is not able to care for him/herself.
- ❑ Someone I loved has just died or left me.
- ❑ I am retired.
- ❑ I have money problems.
- ❑ I am an adolescent/child experiencing school or family problems.

If you checked at least two boxes in each of the three categories, chances are you are suffering from burnout. The more boxes you checked, the more severe your burnout is likely to be.

Chapter One

Why Society Is Burning Out

The American Dream — to overcome obstacles, to accomplish and to succeed — has been tenderly passed from generation to generation, evolving into our most basic symbol of self-reliance and self-indulgence. Our culture is driven by the American Dream, with its basic assumption that everyone can be classified as either a success or a failure based on his or her acquisition of money and material rewards. This value system has no tolerance for less-tangible achievements: There are only winners and losers.

Yet, the reality is that this ambitious cultural, societal and individual standard is becoming less and less attainable by most Americans today. And the resultant stress of striving for a goal that is always out of reach, and therein being branded as a failure, lays the foundation for burnout.

A related and centrally important aspect is that our self-identity has come to be defined solely in terms of outside validation. Our opinion of ourselves is based on what others think of us! We attribute a great deal of value to the perceptions our friends, family and neighbors hold of us — what they think about our jobs and earnings, about how hard we work, and the extent and quality of the material goods we've managed to accumulate.

The traditional American family of a working father who brings home the bacon and a mother who stays home and takes care of the two kids is fading rapidly into our cultural memory.

At the same time, the American home no longer provides the idealized sanctuary that it once did. The traditional American family of a working father who brings home the bacon and a mother who stays home and takes care of the two kids is fading rapidly into our cultural memory. Households are increasingly headed by a single, working parent, and in most of the intact families both parents must work due to economic necessity. In short, our preconceived concepts of marriage and family are no longer relevant or accurate, and not having a set "role" or function in our family relationships often leads to more uncertainty and more stress.

As a result of these stressors, as we shall see, burnout can, and does, affect individuals from all walks of life and from all social strata — from blue collar workers to corporate executives, flight attendants to hospital nurses, long-distance truckers to college professors. Burnout cuts across all family types and social roles, with everyone from homemakers to executives, and children to senior citizens, as potential victims. The common denominator is that we all face a world that is faster, more tension-packed, and generally more exhausting than in the so-called "Golden Years" that exist now only in American myth.

Who's at Fault?

While it's often possible to identify the factors that lead to burnout in any specific case, the common tendency is to blame that catch-all bogey man, *stress*, as the cause of burnout. This diagnosis is simplistic. Do we blame the weatherman when a heat wave occurs, or the seismologist for an earthquake? Going out of our way to find someone or something to blame should be seen for what it is — a sign of *denial!*

Nevertheless, the natural inclination is to look for a guilty party — someone or something to take the responsibility for our problems. Succumbing to burnout is perceived as so shameful that we feel compelled to hang the blame somewhere to avoid seeming weak or flawed. Workers blame employers, children blame neglectful parents and spouses blame insensitive partners. Others take a broader perspective and blame society in general or identify some esoteric scapegoat (perhaps the federal government or Japan). Ultimately, however, such efforts to find someone or something to blame are only excuses to avoid taking responsibility for our own unhappiness.

In actuality, we spend much of our lives in the "automatic mode," living from day to day, not paying enough attention to the real content of our experiences. Many of us continue this way for years, with the underlying tensions and contradictions building up. Then, for some reason, a red flag goes up and we realize *something is wrong*. As the situation nears crisis, we step back and ask ourselves: *What went wrong? Who's doing this to me?*

What we fail to recognize is that, while our stressors may certainly be external and real, we have willingly bought into the mind-set that allows them to affect us. Our single-minded quest to acquire material goods and our inordinate desire to impress or please others have blinded us to our internal sense of meaning, purpose and values. Our own behaviors can, and do, contribute to our pain.

Succumbing to burnout is perceived as so shameful that we feel compelled to hang the blame somewhere to avoid seeming weak or flawed.

What We Can Do

Many "How to Overcome..." books pose nebulous standards of physical and mental health, and even more vague methods for attaining it. Favored approaches include elementary prompting, fad techniques and hypnotic regression. Many of these methods of "un-stressing" assume that burnout victims are already aware of their own contribution to the problem — or that such an awareness is not really necessary.

Nothing could be further from the truth! Awareness of our own role in the burnout process is absolutely necessary if we are to cope effectively with our situation and defuse the burnout process. Further, if we were to simply incorporate all of the faddish self-help methods into our daily lives without a full understanding of our own condition, all we would achieve would be to compress ourselves into an even smaller psychological box than the one already trapping us.

The logical steps in solving any problem, be it emotional, psychological or occupational, consist of *recognition, confrontation, feedback* and, ultimately, *identification* and *implementation* of solutions. If we stop at recognition, or recognition never comes at all, the result is likely to be a growing sense of career and life dissatisfaction punctuated by overwhelming feelings of personal futility, despair, discouragement and disillusionment.

One of the most important messages in this book is that, as we trudge through our daily life, our defenses, especially denial, are so strongly developed that we rarely recognize the early signs of burnout. It often takes a catastrophic event or a huge backlog of frustration before we realize that something is wrong. Unfortunately, by the time the burnout process has reached that point, it is all the more difficult to take corrective action.

The goal of this book is, first, to explain the nature of burnout, and, second, to point out ways to prevent or deal with burnout. Rather than place blame, we will learn to identify and accept our physical and emotional limits, while finding ways to capitalize on our strengths in order to deal more effectively with the stressors in our life and the society within which we live.

> *Awareness of our own role in the burnout process is absolutely necessary if we are to cope effectively with our situation and defuse the burnout process.*

SUMMARY — CHAPTER ONE

Causes of burnout
- ≡ The elusiveness of "The American Dream" — of professional success, wealth and upward mobility
- ≡ A tendency to rely on outside sources to validate our sense of self-worth
- ≡ The radically changed structure of the American family
- ≡ A faster and more tension-packed way of life

Who is suffering
- ≡ Blue collar workers
- ≡ Professionals
- ≡ Homemakers
- ≡ Senior citizens
- ≡ Children/adolescents
- ≡ Almost anyone

Overcoming burnout
- ≡ Become aware of the condition.
- ≡ Accept responsibility — don't shift blame to others or early life experiences.
- ≡ Adjust expectations; set realistic goals.
- ≡ Explore more effective coping behaviors.

Steps to successful problem solving
- ≡ Recognition
- ≡ Confrontation
- ≡ Feedback
- ≡ Identify and implement solutions

Chapter Two

The Myth of the All-American Home

The Sit-com Syndrome

Who or what determines the values of today's American families?

Let's be honest. The scenes depicted by the mass media — television, movies and magazines — are probably the most important factors that determine the values adopted by American families. And this is probably not a very good situation!

It has often been said that art imitates life, but in our society it can be argued that life imitates art in the form of printed and (especially) electronically produced messages. A generation or two ago, the ideal American family was embodied by the Cleavers — Ward, June, Beaver and Wally. Other examples, ranging from "My Three Sons" to "Father Knows Best," represented the unattainable standard to which American families aspired. Those of us who were around in the '50s and '60s wanted to be like those ideal TV families, but never quite seemed to live up to the oh-so-perfect televised images, most of them in situation comedies (sit-coms) that made us laugh without having to think.

Today's televised model family is just as unrealistic, if not more so. Perhaps they cope with more contemporary issues, but, in the end, no problem is too great to be solved in a half hour. For too many American families, not being able to emulate these idealized families, whether they be the Cleavers or the Huxtables, is to admit failure. What every family is supposed to want are those images displayed on the flickering screen, ranging from warm inter-family relationships to a wealth of material goods.

It's not really surprising that family burnout begins to occur when the media's unrealistic image of the "typical American family" fails to reflect the true makeup of American family life.

Family burnout begins to occur when the media's unrealistic image of the "typical American family" fails to reflect the true makeup of American family life.

What Is Today's Family Unit Really Like?

There are over 9 million single parents in America today. Nearly one-third of America's children are raised by a single parent. So, how can a child being raised by a lower-middle-class working mother, for example, relate to those fantasy images being projected into his or her home daily?

Another third of America's population consists of retired persons. Again, this raises the question: Why isn't this important segment of the population represented in the media in ways other than stereotypical old codgers or doting grannies?

Distortion also occurs with regard to ethnic composition. Where are the role models for African-American, Latino or Asian families? Are any role models at all being developed for these groups, or are they expected to react and respond to their portrayal as simply darker-skinned versions of the idealized white TV families that never existed in the first place?

Many of America's minority populations have waited over 20 years, from the early days of television, before being portrayed as principals in even a single family show. Even then, shows such as "The Jeffersons" were largely spin-offs of white-oriented shows. This was predictable, given the fact that the majority of the writers of those shows were of the same race — white!

All of this denial of reality by the media feeds our own inadequacy when we don't "measure up." The influences that shape our families from the outside are the ones that seek to exploit the family! Even more seductive than the sit-com family are advertisements on television and elsewhere that create images that are too attractive to resist, attempting to convince us — particularly teenagers and young adults — that what they are selling is truly irresistible. For many, viewing these images leads to frustration, since obtaining such an array of material goods is rarely feasible or practical.

How does the reality of our lives relate to the images we see on television? Not closely at all, and the gap is widening. For example, in 1955, 60 percent of American families consisted of a biological father who worked, and a biological mother who stayed at home taking care of the children. Today, only 11 percent of the nation's families fit this pattern.

How does the reality of our lives relate to the images we see on television? Not closely at all, and the gap is widening.

More than half of all American marriages end in divorce, and this means that more than half of America's 52 million children under age 18 spend part of their lives in single-parent households. Unlike television, most live with their mothers, and many of the mothers find it difficult to maintain a financially adequate lifestyle. Additionally, approximately half of America's two-parent households are "blended" or stepparent families. It is safe to say that most do not resemble the "Brady Bunch."

Additionally, it is quite common for a lonely parent or parents to become pathologically dependent on their children — as a source of emotional gratification or stability — and this serves to stunt the child's normal independence. Other parents displace anger, frustration and aggression about stressful events in their lives, such as problems in the workplace, onto their children, often becoming abusive, neglectful or both.

The Fundamental Question

Who or what determines the values of today's American families? It is important to develop a fuller understanding of what our concept of family means to us, as well as what it represents in our lives. Rediscovering the importance of family, particularly in relation to our jobs and work lives, is essential if we hope to balance our physical, mental and spiritual needs. But our assessments and expectations must be realistic — not based on how our families "measure up" to media stereotypes or cultural myths.

Learning to understand and de-emphasize the unrealistic role models that dominate our culture and personal lives is essential if we are to succeed in meeting our long-term goals — and avoid becoming burned out!

Rediscovering the importance of family, particularly in relation to our jobs and work lives, is essential if we hope to balance our physical, mental and spiritual needs.

CASE HISTORY   Susan T.

Susan T., a 41-year-old real estate broker and single parent, didn't want to leave the company she worked for, because she loved her job. Yet, she also recognized that her obsession with her work was in direct conflict with the rest of her life.

"I over-identified with my job. It was part of my life. I almost always brought work home with me, and it really affected my ability to be a good parent. I had a lot of physical stress, things like panic attacks and stomach problems. The razzing from the men (the male sales agents at work) was constant and incredible. It was affecting my identity, and I kept asking myself: Am I a woman? A mother? A successful real estate broker? What?

"I reached a point where I literally had a breakdown. I found myself on the floor crying hysterically one day, afraid that I was losing my mind. I denied it and denied it, and just went on with my job. I would take more aspirin for the headaches, more antacids for the stomach problems. Every day I was so exhausted that it was all I could do to drag myself home and crawl into bed at the end of the day.

"I was angry at my body for failing me. I was angry that I couldn't face the denial of my emotional pain.

"Finally, however, I was able to deal with it all. It's taken five hard years, but now I've rebuilt my life. I realized that I had over-identified with the image of the successful broker, and that it wasn't really what I wanted to be. I went back to school and earned a bachelor's degree in psychology. My children were really happy I was home. I found a new balance in my life, and I'm now working toward my master's degree in social work."

SUMMARY — CHAPTER TWO

The "Sit-com Syndrome"
≡ Families on TV are tightly knit and invariably loving and understanding.
≡ No one has money, health or job worries.
≡ Families are mostly upper-middle-class whites, or, if not, are stereotyped or "imitation-white" ethnics.
≡ Problems are minor, and can be solved in a half hour.

The reality of today's family
≡ There are 9 million single parents.
≡ A third of the population is retired.
≡ Only 11 percent of families consist of a biological father and a mother who stays home with the children.
≡ African-Americans, Latinos and Asians make up a significant portion of the population, and contribute a wide variety of cultural heritages.
≡ More than half of all marriages end in divorce.
≡ Half of all children will live in single-parent homes and/or have a stepparent.
≡ Lonely parents may become pathologically dependent on their children or vent their frustration about other aspects of their lives on them.

Chapter Three

Who's Confused About Sex Roles? Almost Everybody!

Sex Roles and the Family

Individual and family problems often go hand in hand. The stressed-out family member is likely to act out his or her tensions in the family setting, putting additional pressure on others in the family. Many parents, for example, react to their stressful situation by becoming more rigid and dogmatic in their communication style, barking responses such as, "Don't do as I do, do as I say," and "Just follow orders!"

Women are particularly vulnerable, as they try to juggle their various roles. Traditionally, when a problem arose at home, responsibility for dealing with it was assumed by the non-working mother. Today, the economic demands placed on any family are substantial, particularly given our tendency to live beyond our means (the over-utilized credit card). One result is that both parents usually work, and family problem-solving is — at least in theory — shared by both parents. However, while many men give lip service to the ideal of being an equal partner in the area of housework and child rearing, few really practice what they preach. In reality, most women in two-career households still end up carrying the bulk of the load when it comes to running the home and family. This "superwoman" role is loaded with stress and frustration. The woman who has difficulty coping with the numerous demands on her may begin to experience difficulties in relationships with mates, children and co-workers.

Why Women Are More Depressed

According to an American Psychological Association task force on women and depression, females are twice as likely as men to suffer from depression. Among the task force's findings were that:

Females are twice as likely as men to suffer from depression — one in every four women will suffer clinical depression in her lifetime.

○ One in every four women will suffer clinical depression in her lifetime. But as many as half of all cases may never be diagnosed or may be misdiagnosed.

○ Females account for 58 percent of all visits to doctors, and take 73 percent of all mood-altering (psychotropic) medications. This proportion increases to 90 percent when the prescribing physician is not a psychiatrist.

○ The suicide rate among professional women is rising, with the rate now being as high for females as it is for males.

There are many reasons why women are so prone to depression, including:

○ Males and females use and experience love relationships quite differently, with females being more sensitive to the ups and downs in interpersonal relationships than men.

○ Financial difficulties, victimization, perceived lack of control over one's life and repressed anger are all associated with depression.

- Marital problems were reported as the most common cause of depression among women in therapy. While marriage tends to reduce a man's risk of depression, women in unhappy marriages are far more likely than men to be depressed.
- Mothers of young children are especially vulnerable to depression. The more children in the home, the more likely the mother is to be depressed.
- The rate of sexual and physical abuse of females is much higher than previously suspected, and as many as one in three women may be victims of abuse by age 21.
- Poverty is a "pathway to depression" for women, and women and children comprise 75 percent of the American population living in poverty.
- Cognitive and personality styles such as avoidance, passivity, dependence, pessimism, negativity and focusing on depressed feelings make depression more likely.

One of the more painful facts uncovered by the APA task force is that depression in women can be remarkably persistent — over half of all women with depression reported that they still had symptoms nine years later. There is hope, however, that the illness, characterized by a debilitating sense of hopelessness and sadness, can be successfully treated in 80 percent to 90 percent of cases using a combination of drugs and personal therapy.

Depression can be successfully treated in 80 percent to 90 percent of cases using a combination of drugs and personal therapy.

Cultural Mythology and Men's Stress

There is a deeply ingrained myth in our culture that men are supposed to act, feel and express themselves in a certain way. Men are conditioned from early childhood not to express their feelings, to act aggressively and to never show vulnerability or fear. These unrealistic societal expectations ulti-

Men are conditioned from early childhood not to express their feelings, to act aggressively and to never show vulnerability or fear. These unrealistic societal expectations ultimately take a significant toll.

mately take a significant toll, both physically and psychologically.

The pressures on contemporary men are intense, as evidenced in a recent report by the Department of Health and Human Services that highlighted the various ways that American men are dying. For example, the death rate for men from heart disease was 229.6 for every 100,000 men, as compared to a rate of only 121.7 per 100,000 among women. Similar differentials exist for cirrhosis of the liver and deaths from violence.

The pressures are felt significantly by men from ages 25 to 34 years. Accidents, suicides and homicides were the most frequent causes of death for both men and women in this age group. The percentage of deaths attributed to suicide was higher for males (13 percent) than females (eight percent), and this was also true for deaths caused by homicides (12 percent for males versus nine percent for females).

Perhaps most at risk are men between the ages of 35 and 44 years. Their cumulative death rate of 318.2 per 100,000 is more than twice the rate of 150.6 for females in the same age group!

It seems that our culture pushes men towards death-defying behavior as a way of proving their manhood. Men push themselves to their limits mentally and physically, embracing death-defying behaviors with gusto. But that's not really death-defying at all; it's death-inviting.

In short, men today are faced with substantial challenges in balancing their family and professional roles. Even if the man is committed to equality with his spouse, businesses are often reluctant to allow the father to act as a parent. Men hesitate to ask for time off to deal with a family problem, knowing that their bosses assume that to be the mother's role. ("Let your wife take the time off work, Harry. We need you!")

Challenges for America's Youth

The rapidly shifting social environment has also led to massive changes in the perceptions and attitudes held by today's youth. According to one recent survey, nearly 75 percent of teenagers (both male and female) thought it would be difficult or impossible for them to have a successful marriage. An astounding 85 percent also felt that members of their generation, compared to their parents, would be more likely to divorce.

Today's youth also have a much different perspective about having families of their own. Most respondents to the survey felt that having children would come much later in marriage, primarily after a viable career had been established. Many of today's younger generation perceive the Baby Boomers — now in their 40s and early 50s — as being primarily motivated by career and the need to make money. In contrast, they worry more about having a happy marriage and raising well-adjusted children. In essence, they seem to be saying: "The generation before us lost itself in materialism. We don't want to repeat their mistakes!"

At the same time, American youth are also threatened by the constant stress and pressure generated by our society. In fact, according to a recently released report by the Centers for Disease Control, over a quarter of American high school students have, at some point, thought seriously about killing themselves! This startling statistic gives us a clue that all is not right with American youth.

Over a quarter of American high school students have, at some point, thought seriously about killing themselves!

Sex Roles in the Workplace

America's business communities continue to trail behind other segments of society in recognizing the need to abandon old sex-role stereotypes within the workplace.

It is true that there has been an extraordinary growth in the representation of women in a wide variety of managerial occupations. Women now constitute 40 percent of workers in executive, administrative and managerial occupations, compared to 20 percent in 1972 and 30 percent in 1980.

However, many critics have also observed that women's progress has been largely in less-desirable and less-compensated occupations — those with less status attached. Median weekly wages for female full-time workers reached 71 percent of wages received by males in comparable positions in the third quarter of 1990, the highest they have ever been. This blatantly unequal compensation remains a primary source of stress and frustration for today's working female.

Women's progress has been largely in less-desirable and less-compensated occupations — those with less status attached. This blatantly unequal compensation remains a primary source of stress and frustration for today's working female.

Additionally, women employees are expected to cheerfully and professionally carry out support or "grunt" work. Even women who work their way up to the executive suite tend to buy into the stereotype that the menial work of the office should be performed by other females. Women seeking role models or mentors from the population of women who have "made it" may be frustrated by an "every woman for herself" attitude that exists at the top of many organizations, in that many successful female executives are obsessed with protecting their positions at all costs.

The image of "supermom" is well known — the working woman who somehow manages to hold down a full-time job to help pay the mortgage and provide security, be a wonderful mother and an adoring wife, become involved with worthy causes and still find time for herself without coming apart at the seams. Juggling these multiple and challenging responsibilities has come to be accepted as the norm, even for the single mother who is the sole provider for her children.

Men are also under constant pressure — to produce, to be creative, to improve the organization's bottom line, and to show the boss "what they're made of." At the same time, men are not machines, and must also juggle their occupational roles with their family responsibilities. As an ever-increasing proportion of American women work outside the home, fathers are increasingly pressured by their wives to assume more responsibility for the household and the children. Divorced fathers may have sole custody or shared responsibility for their children. These fathers face the conflicting demands of career and the role of "Mr. Mom."

Few employers, however, recognize the implications of these broad social changes. They maintain that mothers should handle family problems, while fathers should give top priority to their jobs. There have even been recent debates and lawsuits about granting men paternity leave. Female employees are frequently stereotyped by employers as being less stable and more likely to get pregnant, marry and leave the job. (Labor turnover statistics do tend to support this, indicating that the primary cause for women leaving their jobs is to fulfill child-care demands.)

Over 80 percent of parents would like to see employers offer working parents more flexible work schedules and opportunities to do more of their work at home. Recently, a major utility company spokesperson stated, "The replacement of rigidity with flexibility has served the employees well. The premise now is that there is life before and after office hours." This is a step in the right direction!

As an ever-increasing proportion of American women work outside the home, fathers are increasingly pressured by their wives to assume more responsibility for the household and the children. Few employers recognize the implications of these broad social changes.

CASE HISTORY   Theresa L.

Theresa L. a 34-year-old police officer, was highly motivated in her career, and took great pride in her contributions to the community. Yet the stress involved in her work setting almost destroyed her.

"I was a police officer for 10 years, the only female in a 36-man department. For nine years I handled cases of domestic violence, child abuse and sexual assault. I wasn't permitted to engage in patrol activity, even though my evaluations were excellent and I kept requesting patrol duty. I still felt like I was being cheated.

"At first, I denied that job stress was causing any family problems, but I gradually realized that pressure and resentment on the job was pushing me away from my kids. I became depressed, and experienced feelings of despair and grief related to my work. I got real paranoid and thought everyone was watching me all the time.

"Eventually I had to get help. I saw a counselor and began taking anti-depressant medication. I took a leave of absence, but things weren't any better when I returned. I went into a deep depression and was placed on long-term disability. I was really just an emotional wreck. Worst of all, I felt like I had failed and let my community down. I had always felt I could make a difference, but now I had lost all my self-esteem.

"Because of the futility of changing the stressful work conditions, I left the department. This was a major crisis in my life. I was forced to give up everything I had worked for and wanted. I filed a Workers' Compensation claim and concentrated on becoming more active in my family. I want to regain a more positive self-image and deal with my depression. My therapist tells me that time will play a major factor in getting me through this crisis in my life."

SUMMARY — CHAPTER THREE

Women and depression

≡ One in four women will suffer clinical depression in her lifetime.

≡ Up to half of all cases of depression are undiagnosed or misdiagnosed.

≡ Women account for 58 percent of visits to doctors and take 73 percent of all mood-altering medications.

≡ Females are generally more sensitive to interpersonal relationships.

≡ Mothers often assume the bulk of care for young children, a task that is associated with depression.

≡ Women and children account for 75 percent of all Americans living below the poverty line.

≡ Women earn, on the average, 71 percent of what men earn for comparable jobs.

≡ Women are more likely to have support or "grunt" type jobs.

≡ It may be difficult for women to find "mentors" willing to give career guidance.

≡ The "supermom" image sets impossible standards.

≡ Women may rely more on cognitive styles such as avoidance, passivity, dependence, pessimism and negativity — all related to depression.

Men's stress

≡ Men are conditioned to repress emotions, act aggressively and never show vulnerability or fear.

≡ Men are much more likely to suffer from heart disease, cirrhosis of the liver and death by violence or suicide.

≡ The workplace discourages men from taking time off to participate in family life, nevertheless, there is increasing pressure from their wives to do so.

≡ Divorced fathers may have full custody or, at the least, childcare responsibilities during visitations.

≡ Society encourages men to define their success in terms of work and earnings.

Pressures on young people

≡ Today's teenagers are discouraged about their future chances for career success and marital happiness.

≡ Children are growing up in broken homes or blended families.

≡ Child abuse is on the increase.

≡ Over a quarter of American high school students have considered suicide.

Chapter Four

The Human Arson in Our Schools

Stress and Frustration Among Educators

The crisis facing educators today is very real. Ironically, the largest budget cuts nationally have been in education, while the largest increases in expenditures are for the building of new prisons! Revenues are being severely restricted, with school districts throughout the nation being forced to cut services across the board. Teacher layoffs are common, with remaining staff teaching ever-larger class loads. Administrative and support personnel are being eliminated, and desperately needed special programs and services are usually the first to go.

A Generation of Illiterates

These reductions in the capability of our educational system have reached epidemic proportions in recent years. The social impact is made even more serious by other factors in our society that are impacting American children — broken homes,

At the very time when our educational system could play a central role in counteracting the negative effects of broad social trends, such as broken homes, abuse and neglect and lack of family rootedness, it has been undermined.

abuse and neglect, lack of family rootedness and electronic media — especially television. At the very time when our educational system could play a central role in counteracting the negative effects of these broad social trends, it has been undermined. With class size increasing, teachers can no longer provide individual instruction. Instead, they tend to issue passing marks to most students just to expedite their passage through today's assembly line educational system.

According to the U.S. Department of Education:

o An estimated 25 million Americans — one in 10 — are illiterate.
o Dropout rates exceed 25 percent nationally and 50 percent in urban centers. Rates are even higher among minority youth.
o Americans rank 15th of 16 nations in terms of teenagers' scientific knowledge.

According to a recent study of 2,000 randomly selected adults of all ages, only 18 percent could decipher a bus schedule, and barely 40 percent could calculate the correct change from a $3 restaurant bill! Only one-third could determine the correct dose of medicine to give a child by using a dosage chart based on the child's weight and age.

Individuals who choose to pursue a career in education are faced with tremendous stressors and frustrations. There seems to be no end to the personal and professional demands on educators today. Yet, despite the difficulty and importance of the job, the public perception is that teachers are overpaid and underworked. In fact, teachers' average annual income of $29,000 is far below the income earned by others with comparable educational qualifications. For teachers today, job security is based on budgetary factors rather than on professional talent or dedication. Even those with tenure or tremendous demonstrated ability are no longer protected against an unexpected pink slip.

A recent survey of American teachers revealed a high level of job satisfaction, but also painted a grim and depressing picture of teachers' professional lives. More than half felt that respect for teachers in the community was not what it should be, and that parents' lack of participation in school activities represented a major obstacle to quality education. The survey, with responses from over 22,000 teachers, revealed several other highly disturbing trends. Almost 90 percent of teachers felt that abused and neglected children were an on-going problem for educators. Student absenteeism, apathy and disruptive behavior were cited as making their jobs more demanding.

Not too long ago, the only counselor at a 1,500-student school in the Midwest walked into her office to begin a typical day. Her desk was cluttered with 14 messages from parents and six from students, and she knew that she would have a hard time returning all the calls while still meeting her other, quite-demanding responsibilities. Then she saw an additional message from the school district — a pink slip!

Reflecting on the irony of her situation, the counselor's only comment was, "The small things we as adults can cope with are devastating to kids. I'll be able to find another job, or even another career. The children will be the ones hurt at the end of this."

While the unselfish attitude of this counselor is admirable, the outcome for millions of students is all too discouraging. This story is being repeated across the nation, affecting 150,000 front-line teachers in 1991 alone!

There seems to be no end to the personal and professional demands on educators today. Yet, the public perception is that teachers are overpaid and underworked.

CASE HISTORY   Sarah J.

Sarah J. is a public school teacher who has worked in a lower-socioeconomic school district for 18 years. She sums up some of the frustrations that caused her to experience stress overload.

"Public school teachers have little input into the educational system. We're controlled by an elected board of education, and most of their motivation is political; they have their own agenda. They tell us what to do, when to do it, and how to do it. Even when we go out of our way to follow their directions, they usually come back and tell us we did it wrong.

"In the classroom, I do have some control, but, even there, it's pretty common for the administration to override a teacher. You can register all the complaints you want, but all they say is: 'No. No. No. It doesn't work that way. This is how you have to do it.'

"As for the students, you'd never believe some of the problems they bring to the classroom. It's easy to say 'Educate them — teach them.' But you can't teach children who haven't eaten. Too many kids come from homes where they've been abused physically, mentally or sexually. Many don't even have a home. They're shifted around from one parent to another parent, from one relative to another relative. What they really need, of course, is love and attention, but it's hard for teachers to give that all the time."

CASE HISTORY   George H.

George H., an educator with over 20 years experience, speaks seven languages and frequently provides translation for corporations and private agencies. While his first love is teaching, he is having second thoughts about how long he can continue to perform effectively as a teacher.

"Teaching is different today than it used to be. Kids are uncontrollable, with no respect for teachers, and come to school with guns and knives. Each term I'm threatened with physical harm a dozen times, and know that a violent incident can occur at any time. These problems originate in the kids' homes. A lot of their families are just out of balance. On parents' night, we're lucky if one out of 10 parents show up. It's like they don't care. They send their kids to school because they have to. Sometimes I feel like there should be a law requiring parents to spend time at the school to see what we go through.

"The environment at school has to be even more terrifying for the straight kids trying to make something out of themselves. They're the ones I care about and the reason I teach.

"And then there's the monetary aspect. I have to consult to make ends meet. The money we make is so much less than other comparable occupations. Funds for education are being cut everywhere. Frankly, it looks to most teachers like the American people don't give a damn. They want quality education for their kids, but they're not willing to pay for it.

"I do my job because I love teaching. It takes a particular kind of person to teach, and not everyone can do it. I love doing it, but I really don't know how long I'll be able to put up with the downside. The stress and pressure never let up, and I'm asking myself whether it's worth it for me to continue in this profession."

A Five-point Plan to Alleviate Educator Stress

Most educators function not only as teachers, but also as a parent, friend and disciplinarian to a broad range of culturally diverse students.

America's teachers are faced with tremendous challenges and equally tremendous levels of stress. Most function not only as teacher, but also as parent, friend and disciplinarian to a broad range of culturally diverse students. While they are faced with an uncertain professional future, they are not exempt from their own family and relationship problems as well.

Not surprisingly, this load can become overwhelming for many, if not most, teachers. As one physician who specializes in treating stress among educators put it, "I repeatedly see teachers who have panic attacks, tension headaches, and who chronically become despondent on Sunday nights in anticipation of their coming work week."

Educators who are becoming overwhelmed by tension and stress might consider a simple five-point plan such as the following:

o Develop an active social life with those who are not professional educators. Don't talk shop during leisure time.

o Organize support groups at work to share feelings and insights about common problems. Sharing ideas and approaches in this manner reduces stress and keeps it where it belongs!

o Exercise! Regular physical exercise helps release much of the tension experienced each day. Educators have a tendency to be sedentary in their work and personal lives, and a well-balanced physical fitness program is most beneficial.

o Minimize the amount of work taken home. If additional hours are required to complete work, try to spend them at work, not at home. Teachers must respect their personal limits and be considerate of the needs of their families. Remember, maintaining balance between work and home is essential for a healthy life.

o Seek professional help should it become necessary. If stress becomes overwhelming, consider talking with a professional counselor.

Education and Business — A Perfect Marriage?

We've lost something else in many of our schools besides discipline. We've lost the value of failure. The first thing some youngsters flunk these days is life itself. That's because they've been passed from one grade to another, and eventually graduated, even though they've been failing at every step. The only problem is, nobody's told them. In attempting to shield these kids from failure, we've guaranteed it.

— Lee Iacocca

There has been considerable discussion in recent years about the need for the business community to become more involved with education, especially now that responsibility for some programs has shifted from the national to the local level. Keith Geiger, past president of the National Education Association, advocates such a move. While he argues that the business world shouldn't tell educators how to run the schools, he also points out that business and education have gone in opposite directions for far too long.

Business could fund programs to make students and parents more aware of the value of education in the labor market. Explaining the purpose and value of education to students and concretely demonstrating the benefits of completing an

Business and education have gone in opposite directions for far too long. Business could fund programs to make students and parents more aware of the value of education in the labor market.

education could motivate students to stay in school and help alleviate the heavy burden on teachers, counselors and administrators.

Corporate America spends large sums of money, estimated at between $50 and $200 billion annually, on training and educational programs. The largest spender is IBM, which has an annual training budget of $2 billion. It is logical that corporations with well-developed training facilities should consider making those facilities available to help ease the burdens on our educational system. One model is provided by Aetna Life and Casualty in Connecticut, which trains close to 30,000 students a year. The company has made its training facility available on weekends to provide educational programs for inner-city youths.

Corporations with well-developed training facilities should consider making those facilities available to help ease the burdens on our educational system.

Examples of corporate involvement in education:

o The Chrysler Corporation's sponsorship, to the tune of $5 million, of *Learning in America* for the MacNeil/ Lehrer News Hour.
o American Express has created the National Academy Foundation to support academies in public schools.
o Corporate community school sponsorship by companies such as Quaker Oats, Burger King, Whirlpool, Dow Chemical, as well as concerned public figures such as Oprah Winfrey.

Ultimately, school-business partnerships must be established across the nation. The chief complaint of the business community is that employees entering their doors are educationally ill-equipped, and it is up to the business community to help develop a plan for dealing with the problem. Some potentially valuable alternatives include:

The chief complaint of the business community is that employees entering their doors are educationally ill-equipped.

- Establish scholarship programs.
- Sponsor visits to corporate training centers for teachers and school administrators.
- Offer summer and part-time employment for teachers and students.
- Host field trips to businesses, museums, science centers, college campuses.
- Underwrite the cost of computers and other information processing equipment.
- Establish funding for new school buildings and the renovation of older ones.

Other countries such as Japan and Germany are already implementing proposals such as these. If the United States would follow suit, it would provide the necessary link between education and the business community that has been significantly lacking thus far.

Summary — Chapter Four

The decline in education
≡ One in 10 Americans is illiterate.
≡ High school dropout rates exceed 25 percent — 50 percent in urban centers.
≡ American teenagers rank 15th out of 16 nations in scientific knowledge.

Teachers' stress
≡ Teachers may be laid off at a moment's notice.
≡ There is a shortage of money for textbooks, supplies and educational aids.
≡ Class size has increased dramatically.
≡ Student absenteeism, apathy and disruptive behavior are on the rise.

Solutions from corporate America
≡ Businesses could fund programs teaching the value of education in the labor market.
≡ Many businesses have training programs and facilities already in place that could be adapted to students' needs.
≡ Scholarship programs could be established.
≡ Students and teachers alike would benefit from summer and part-time employment.
≡ Business could host educational field trips, provide computer equipment and build and renovate school facilities.

Chapter Five

Fear and Loathing in the American Workplace

There is nothing sacred about tradition....The brain carries the memory of yesterday, which is tradition, and is frightened to let go, because it cannot face something new. Tradition becomes our security; and when the mind is secure, it is in decay.

— *Krishnamurti*

In today's hectic world, it makes little difference what we do for a living or even where we work — burnout does not discriminate! One survey of 1,000 business people clearly reflects the predominance of potential stress in our workplaces and the imbalance in many workers' lives:

○ 85 percent work more than 45 hours a week.
○ 81 percent experience stress; 48 percent on a daily basis.
○ 89 percent take work home with them.
○ 65 percent work more than one weekend a month.

Across the nation, the fastest-growing category of disability claims reported by employees is classified as "anxiety reactions and mental disorders." While no single data source accurately reflects the true incidence of occupational illness and disability among today's work force, there are some fascinating and highly suggestive statistics. In one state alone, 7,650 stress claims were filed in 1990, resulting in $370 million in benefits paid. Additionally, from 1980 to 1988, claims for mental stress among public sector employees increased five-fold! Of these, approximately 11 percent of all county government indemnity cases were attributed to stress, making up nearly 30 percent of the total expenditures on Workers' Compensation claims. The cost to insurance carriers and self-insured cities statewide was close to $70 million in benefits paid!

Today's workplace is characterized by both a greater frequency and longer duration of exposure to stress. More tasks must be handled, and deadlines are increasingly shorter.

Today's workplace is characterized by both a greater frequency and longer duration of exposure to stress. At all levels, from top executives to front-line employees, more tasks must be handled, and deadlines are increasingly shorter. The unrelenting pressure to increase productivity has created "...a feverish pace that seems to have emerged in the last three to five years," according to Edward Sanford, chairman of Pepperdine University's Economics, Marketing and Quantitative Methods Department.

Every work environment has characteristics that create the potential for stress, anxiety and crisis. At the same time, our internal or personality factors create or intensify our emotional distress.

According to the California Workers' Compensation Institute, disabilities involving mental stress increased by an amazing 700 percent between 1979 and 1988, while disabling physical work injuries of all types increased by only 17 percent. Women accounted for two-thirds of all mental stress claims. Other important facts:

o The number of mental stress claims may be nearly four times greater than previously reported — perhaps as many as 30,000 stress claims in 1987.

o Nine out of 10 stress claimants received Workers' Compensation benefits.

o Fewer than 10 percent of all mental stress claims stem from a single incident — most are attributed to cumulative events.

o "Job pressures" caused nearly seven out of 10 stress claims, while "harassment" was cited in one-third of the claims.

Instability in the Workplace

A major factor contributing to the American stress epidemic is the wave of restructuring and cost-cutting that has swept corporate America during the past decade. The bottom-line drive to stay competitive has forced companies to let employees go, redistributing their responsibilities among the remaining workers.

Many organizations treat stress purely on a crisis intervention basis, only acknowledging it when an employee becomes dysfunctional. A better solution would be to implement programs that directly address stress-causing environmental and occupational factors. Employers are slowly recognizing that preventing stress-related disorders among employees *is* cost effective.

Occupational and Organizational Stress Factors

A primary source of workplace stress relates to our own expectations of what we hope to get out of our jobs. Often, we do not feel adequately recognized or respected at work, and instead experience constant frustrations in dealing with management. When personality conflicts go unresolved, or when workloads are too heavy and disproportionate to credit received, it is inevitable that we feel "trapped in the rat race." Employees need to receive credit for the work they do. When

A primary source of workplace stress relates to our own expectations of what we hope to get out of our jobs. Often, we do not feel adequately recognized or respected at work, and experience constant frustrations.

Employees need to receive credit for the work they do. When such credit isn't given, feelings of resentment, anger, bitterness, vindictiveness and sometimes even hatred are the likely result.

such credit isn't given, feelings of resentment, anger, bitterness, vindictiveness and sometimes even hatred are the likely result.

Certain aspects of the work environment have been shown to contribute to the stress level of employees:

- Numerous responsibilities, but little authority in decision-making
- Insufficient time to satisfactorily complete tasks
- Unclear expectations (lack of a clear job description)
- Absence of a clearly defined chain of command
- No recognition or reward for a job well done
- Lack of opportunity to voice complaints
- Incompatibility with superiors, co-workers or subordinates due to differences in personality, values or goals
- Lack of control over, or pride in, the finished product
- Job insecurity due to the possibility of layoffs, takeovers, mergers, closures or relocations (especially prevalent in our current recession)
- Prejudice and discrimination based on age, gender, race, sexual orientation or religion
- Unpleasant environmental conditions — crowding, noise, exposure to chemicals or smoke, commuting difficulties, inadequate or non-working equipment
- Inability to apply personal abilities effectively or fulfill potential
- Problems at home — family worries, financial problems, alcohol/drug/gambling problems, etc.
- The "FUD Factor" — fear, uncertainty and doubt

Why Some Managers Fail

In today's highly competitive world, the demands made on corporate executives have soared to incredible levels. They are told that they must cut costs and downsize operations yet still increase productivity. This has led to an upsurge of "get-tough" approaches in dealing with employees at all levels. Many executives feel that their employees are "too comfortable"; they are focused exclusively on the bottom line. This leads to a strictly results-oriented approach, with little concern for how much the effort costs the employees.

Corporate executives are told that they must cut costs and downsize operations yet still increase productivity. This leads to the "get tough" approach.

However, increasing numbers of these "tough-guy" executives are coming to realize that this management style entails certain risks — it demoralizes valuable employees by making them feel unappreciated and drives relatively poor performers to commit acts of sabotage against the company.

Enlightened executives are beginning to implement more proactive and humanistic approaches. Instead of pressuring their employees, they utilize positive strategies such as establishing advisory councils composed of a cross-section of employees. Such councils provide a forum for employees' ideas on saving money and streamlining operations. This orientation helps employees feel like partners with a vested interest in the organization. While the get-tough approach may produce immediate, short-term results, the detrimental long-term effects are likely to be far more costly, both in terms of human suffering and dollars paid for stress-related claims.

While it has always been important for managers to develop interpersonal skills and invest in ongoing education, it is even more necessary today. If the manager's job entails complex communication, personnel and political systems, it is absolutely essential. Today's managers cannot afford to rely on past experience and some vague "innate ability" to make things happen. Instead, they must tap all available personnel and management technology and master communications — both verbal and written — with colleagues, subordinates and superiors.

Companies should encourage management and employees to communicate and work together more effectively. The ideal manager in today's tough corporate environment combines cost-consciousness with creativity and caring.

Companies should encourage management and employees to communicate and work together more effectively. The ideal manager in today's tough corporate environment combines cost-consciousness with creativity and caring.

At the same time, the burnout suffered by workers cannot be blamed totally on their employers. Michael Matteson, professor of Organizational Behavior and Management at the University of Houston, points out that stress is not solely the fault of either the environment or the individual, but is the result of the interaction between the two.

According to a recent survey of top management experts, there are at least five significant reasons that managers fail to effectively supervise their subordinates:

Inability to Get Along

The manager with underdeveloped interpersonal skills is likely to have trouble getting along with subordinates. This may be the single most important reason why managers fail to effectively supervise, especially during the early and middle stages of their careers. Such managers tend to view all conflict as negative, rather than recognizing it for what it is — an unavoidable part of life that must be mediated and managed.

Failure to Adapt to Change

Managers who cling to traditional, outmoded leadership styles are out of place in today's changing workplace.

The "Me-Only" Syndrome

Every manager seeks recognition; when carried to extremes, the result is a focus on "me only." A manager affected by this syndrome cares only about making more money and climbing the corporate ladder. Such an exclusive emphasis on ego satisfaction can harm the entire organization.

Fear of Action

Managers who fear taking action inhibit the growth of new ideas. The fear of jeopardizing their own positions blocks innovation, even though they may recognize that an idea or program is essential for furthering organizational goals.

The Inability to Rebound

Managers who have had failures during the course of their careers may not be able to rebound from temporary setbacks. The fear that they may repeat their earlier failures ends up stunting both their own growth and that of others in the organization.

Managers who fear taking action inhibit the growth of new ideas. The fear of jeopardizing their own positions blocks innovation.

Some Jobs Are More Stressful Than Others

Researchers who have studied the stress levels inherent in various occupations have identified certain occupations as having more than their share of stress:

- Bus drivers
- Teachers
- Ministers, priests
- Firefighters, paramedics and foresters
- Physicians, dentists
- Nurses
- Flight attendants
- Railroad engineers
- Research scientists
- Restaurant managers
- Law enforcement personnel
- Attorneys

CASE HISTORY   Ted R.

Ted R., a veteran firefighter/paramedic, confronts life-and-death situations daily. The traumatic nature of his experiences represents a constant threat to his sense of well-being.

"We were called to a residential fire in the middle of the night. When I learned there were children inside, my stomach tightened. When we entered the house to save the kids, we couldn't see for the smoke, but we finally found a small, limp little girl, and then another. We pulled them out, only to learn that there were more kids inside. The two we'd gotten out weren't breathing, so I tried to save them while my partner looked for the others. While I was giving mouth-to-mouth to them, another four kids were removed; they were lying lifeless on the curb. I desperately tried to save those kids, especially a six-year-old girl (whose name I later learned was Melinda). But it was useless. Melinda lasted the longest, only four days. The other kids died at the scene.

"One of the first things you learn as a firefighter is not to get emotionally involved. But that's just not the kind of person I am. I went to see the family, and the mother showed me a letter Melinda had written about what she wanted in life. It was very moving and emotional.

"About a week later, I woke up from a sound sleep, crying after a nightmare. In the dream, Melinda was lying in bed, bright, shiny and cheerful. She sat in my lap and asked me to tell her about the things she was going to miss in life. I couldn't sleep for nights. I'd come home from work, hug my own kids, and cry and cry. This was the first time this sort of thing had happened to me, and I was afraid I'd 'cracked'; I had always bought into the macho thing and made a big deal about being able to handle anything. I got help, and learned that this was a normal reaction to the stress of what I'd gone through. I'm back at work now, and doing fine, although I still have flashbacks of the experience. And I always remember the anniversary date."

CASE HISTORY   Father O'Hara

A Spritual Light Burned Out

Father O'Hara was a 46-year-old priest. His problems were shaped by his perception of his role as priest and teacher, which gave him his identity. He felt he had to maintain the image of the unflappable, objective "father" at all times. His bottled-up emotions caused his self-esteem to deteriorate and his depression to intensify. After more than 20 years of service to his parish and community, he was placed in a 28-day detoxification program and subsequently forced to retire from the clergy.

"When I first went in for therapy, I told my therapist about how I'd been a well-respected clergy person for almost two decades, and about how I'd been abusing alcohol, marijuana and cocaine for four years. I just couldn't stop on my own.

"My father was a police captain for 26 years, and we always had a lot of conflict. My father was very authoritarian, and always gave me sayings to follow: 'Never bring scandal home,' 'Big boys don't cry' and 'It's effeminate to show emotion.' He never could show any love or outward affection to anyone.

"After I'd been a priest for 15 years, I started to have anxiety attacks and periods of loneliness and deep depression. I saw my parishioners get sick and die. I couldn't do anything except perform last rites and bury them. My parish was mostly older individuals, and each week I buried at least one friend. I felt helpless and isolated most of the time. I kept wanting to sell my home and move to some third-world country to escape the pressure. I didn't do that, but I started killing the pain with alcohol and drugs.

"I started working longer and longer hours. What little personal life I had merged into the professional, and every activity I engaged in was work-related. My guilt, chemical abuse and depression intensified. The spirituality I once had to sustain me during times of distress was replaced by a constant need to stay high to forget my problems."

Clergy Under Siege —
Our Ministers Are Burning Out

That ministers and priests made the list of the most stressful occupations is not surprising. Our spiritual leaders are burning out in ever-increasing numbers. For example, of the $64 million in medical claims for pastors paid by the Southern Baptist Convention in 1990, stress-related illnesses were the second-most-common type of claim (trailing only maternity benefits).

A consultant "conservatively" estimates that 17 percent of the clergy he has worked with over a 20-year period were suffering from long-term stress and burnout.

A senior consultant at a nondenominational organization offering consultation, leadership training and referral services for churches and synagogues "conservatively" estimated that 17 percent of the clergy he has worked with over a 20-year period were suffering from long-term stress and burnout. He defined the burnout he's observed among the clergy as "a disease of the over-committed who refuse to come to terms with their limitations."

As the level of stress in our culture increases, people transfer that pressure to their place of worship and place more demands on clergy. Today's clergy attempts to live up to these expectations by trying to cover all the bases, but it is never enough. Like many others who are employed in the human service professions, they can't seem to quit at the end of the day — there's always someone else in need! As one priest put it:

> *The church was a great place for me to try to get my self-esteem needs met. It seems like many of the priests I know grew up wanting to save our families, especially dysfunctional ones, as in my case, and when that proved impossible, we wanted to save the world. We're generally workaholics. We're great at fixing other people's lives, but we don't have the foggiest notion of what to do for ourselves.*

The director of the C.F. Meninger Memorial Hospital in Topeka, Kansas, a major referral center for troubled clergy, stated, "They try to be loving to others in hopes of getting love in return. Often, to their own surprise, they are met with a host of problems and become the target of complaints, resentment and disappointment."

Evaluating Occupational Stress

Looking beyond the list of jobs considered inherently stressful, data from federal, state and local agencies, as well as the business community, is making it clear that occupational diseases associated with job stress are becoming increasingly common among a broad range of occupations.

Occupational diseases associated with job stress are becoming increasingly common among a broad range of occupations.

Jobs requiring high levels of responsibility yet allowing minimal control have long been thought to be the most stressful. However, a recent study of heart patients also suggests that work demanding vigilance over the well-being of others causes the most stress. It is ironic that the professionals who protect us, guide us spiritually and educate us suffer the most from their work!

Of the nearly 500,000 certified physicians in the United States today, fewer than 1,000 are board-certified in occupational health. This obviously contributes to the inadequate treatment often received for work-related medical problems. Physicians' relative lack of knowledge regarding the negative psychological and physical effects of stressful working environments may also contribute to the probable under-reporting of stress-related illnesses.

General practitioners, internists and other medical professionals who don't specialize in mental health often misdiagnose patients' conditions. A recent Rand Corporation study indicated that doctors failed to recognize severe depression in over 50 percent of their depressed patients!

Stress Reduction in the Workplace — The Role of Management

Business owners, managers and executives have failed to effectively address the problems created by stress in the workplace and the damage that is done to victims. Early recognition of the initial symptoms of stress is essential, as is prompt intervention. Top management must develop a better understanding of our rapidly changing social, political and economic systems.

When an employee at any level is given the best available tools to meet job requirements, one result is enhanced self-esteem and, thus, a healthier work environment.

While keeping up with the latest management techniques is no easy task, it is to the manager's advantage to absorb the new analytical tools that are constantly emerging, as well as mastering today's state-of-the-art communications and computer systems. This knowledge actually diminishes the manager's vulnerability to stress. When an employee at any level is given the best available tools to meet job requirements, one result is enhanced self-esteem and, thus, a healthier work environment.

Many organizations are beginning to sponsor seminars and workshops conducted by outside professionals. Stress-reduction techniques can be integrated as a component of a comprehensive "wellness" program. Useful stress reduction techniques include lectures, education in diet and health management and employee group discussions concerning stress and ways to deal with it. One example: A Boston research lab offers a Tai Chi (Eastern meditation and exercise) class to help workers reduce physical and mental stress.

Teaching employees to recognize the importance of humor on the job is also a highly effective tactic in combating the effects of occupational stress.

Ultimately, all employers should consider implementing an employee assistance program or wellness program emphasizing optimal mental and physical fitness. Whether such a program will succeed or not depends on several interrelated factors:

o Management's awareness and concern regarding the effects of stress
o A firm commitment by management to the wellness program
o Direct management involvement in the program

The financial costs of implementing such programs, while not insubstantial, will be more than offset by benefits in terms of reduced Workers' Compensation stress claims, absenteeism and turnover.

The preservation of the nation's primary resource — the health and welfare of its workers — must be given top priority. Setting such a priority is central to corporate survival. Despite the increased competitiveness in the domestic and international marketplace, this commitment is absolutely essential for the well-being of American workers at all levels. 📖

The preservation of the nation's primary resource — the health and welfare of its workers — must be given top priority.

SUMMARY — CHAPTER FIVE

Workers' stress
- ≡ Almost half of all workers in a survey reported experiencing stress on a daily basis.
- ≡ More than 80 percent worked more than 45 hours a week and took work home.
- ≡ Business today is characterized by more tasks, shorter deadlines and increased demands for productivity.
- ≡ The fastest-growing occupational disability is "anxiety reactions and mental disorders" — most are attributed to cumulative job pressures rather than a single event.
- ≡ Stress can result from inadequate recognition, lack of respect, unresolved personality conflicts and too heavy or disproportionate workloads.

Stressful work situations
- ≡ Numerous responsibilities, little authority
- ≡ Unclear job description
- ≡ Chain of command not clearly defined
- ≡ No recognition or rewards
- ≡ Lack of input
- ≡ Personality conflicts
- ≡ Lack of control over finished product
- ≡ Job insecurity
- ≡ Prejudice
- ≡ Unpleasant work environment
- ≡ Inability to fulfill potential or use personal talents and/or skills

Managers' failure
- ≡ A results-only approach — only the bottom line matters
- ≡ A tough-guy stance

- Poor interpersonal and/or communicative skills
- Failure to adapt to change
- The "Me-Only" syndrome
- Fear of action
- Inability to rebound

Solutions
- A proactive, humanistic approach
- Ongoing education in management techniques
- Advisory councils made up of employees
- Stress reduction seminars and workshops
- Overall wellness programs

Most stressful occupations
- Bus drivers
- Teachers
- Ministers, priests
- Firefighters, paramedics, foresters
- Physicians, dentists, nurses
- Flight attendants
- Railroad engineers
- Research scientists
- Restaurant managers
- Law enforcement personnel
- Attorneys

Stressed-out clergy
- An estimated 17 percent of American clergy suffers from burnout.
- In one denomination, stress-related illnesses were the second most common disability claims paid.

Chapter Six

Retirement — Making a Positive Transition

He who has a why to live can bear with almost any how.
— *Friedrich Nietzsche*

America's Diverse Older Population

There is substantial diversity among the population of older Americans in terms of living situation, economic resources and health. Many retirees live alone or with their spouses. An ever-decreasing number live with their children or close relatives. In areas such as New York and Florida, most retirees live in apartments, using their limited funds to maintain a modest lifestyle.

Retirees who are financially able tend to move to warm climates. Certain geographic areas have larger concentrated populations of retirees than others. For example, New York City has the most retirees, followed by the Sun Belt states of Florida, California and Arizona.

Retirement communities, condominiums and mobile home parks designed for seniors are becoming ever more popular. Many such facilities are well-planned, with appropriate activities and facilities. These types of settings are designed to ease the stress associated with retirement.

However, these same communities can also become "holding tanks" in which seniors are effectively isolated from the rest of society. Many younger adults in our country main-

Many younger adults in our country maintain the attitude of "out of sight, out of mind" with regard to older Americans (including their own parents). Isolation is one of the worst specters of retirement.

tain the attitude of "out of sight, out of mind" with regard to older Americans (including their own parents). Isolation is one of the worst specters of retirement. When the retiree is removed from mainstream society, interaction between younger and older members of the community is precluded. This trend is disturbing, both in terms of the negative effects on isolated seniors and the implications for the younger population — which will, of course, make up the next generation of retirees!

The Economics of Retirement

These are just a few of the questions people ask themselves as they enter their retirement years:

"What am I going to do?"
"Who and where are my friends?"
"Who cares about me?"
"Does anyone understand what is happening to me?"

The stress or anticipatory anxiety associated with retirement actually begins before retirement itself. When we are younger, the concept of retiring is remote and we give it little thought; yet, we also consider it our right to have a decent retirement. As we approach retirement, however, a sense of foreboding and doom may set in as we confront the reality that our working years are coming to an end. Retirement is often thought of in much the same context as death — as the end of our productive life. This causes many of us to avoid discussing or even thinking rationally about our own retirement, let alone planning for how we will handle it. This only serves to make the underlying stress more severe than it need be.

Of primary importance are economic considerations, especially the ability to maintain a comparable standard of living to that of our working years. Many retirees are disappointed to learn that they must settle for far less than they expected. A large proportion of today's retirees have only Social Security benefits to exist on, while others may have small pensions. Even this combination, however, rarely matches the earning power of the middle to later working years. One result is that countless potential retirees have been forced to continue working in order to maintain some semblance of their pre-senior lifestyle.

During the 1950s and 1960s, most homeowners watched their equity grow as property values soared. Now, as retirees, they must deal with the dilemma of wanting to use funds from the sale of their property, in the face of the reality of what they can afford to pay for another home elsewhere.

The Health Care Dilemma

A central issue for today's seniors is the mounting cost of health care. The seemingly uncontrollable rise in cost has doubled Medicare expenditures in the past five years alone, and threatens to bankrupt the separate hospital trust fund by the year 2005.

The seemingly uncontrollable rise in cost has doubled Medicare expenditures in the past five years alone, and threatens to bankrupt the separate hospital trust fund by the year 2005.

There are now more than 33 million recipients of Medicare benefits, and this number continues to increase by about 15 percent annually. Financing for these benefits is becoming quite fragile, and relies primarily on payroll taxes from 138 million workers. It takes the taxes paid by four active workers to pay for the health care costs of each Medicare recipient. The future is bleak, given the current demographic situation. The number of senior citizens will soar as the Baby Boomers age, and it seems quite possible that available funds will be depleted within the next 15 years! If the current system should fail, as many predict it will, seniors will be forced to use their savings or other assets to finance the costs of their own health care.

CASE HISTORY   Martha E.

Martha E. is a 58-year old Hispanic woman who worked for 39 years for a major American insurance company, ending up as an executive manager. In the midst of major cutbacks, she was offered an early retirement package.

"I'd been with the company since I got out of high school, and I always assumed I'd stay with them until retiring at 65. Even though I'd seen some brutal tactics in the business world, I found the coldness that was directed at me hard to take. It was a setup. On the surface they gave me a choice — I could accept the package (a small pension and some severance pay) or accept a demotion to a non-executive job and a freeze in pay until I retired later. The only intelligent choice was to accept the retirement package offered by the company.

"I stayed for six months, but I was filled with resentment and anger. I felt like my loyalty and hard work were being thrown in my face. I'd worked hard to overcome years of discrimination, and had finally reached an executive position. I felt cheated when faced with the loss of my remaining years, which would have been productive both for myself and for the company. The company held seminars to help with the transition, but I wanted no part of them.

"When I left, it was even more of a shock. I had to deal with the disruption of my life routine, and live on two-thirds the income. The tax consequences of early retirement were also terrifying. I had to confront my anger, and that was the hardest part, since it jeopardized my ability to make rational decisions. I turned to a lot of people for help in dealing with this situation. I knew that I just couldn't do it alone.

"You can only do so much gardening, or window-shopping in the mall. Making short-term plans has helped me get through this ordeal. I began to do some volunteer work at a local hospital. Right now, I work in the gift shop, but there are other duties which are more closely related to caretaking and health care which I look forward to doing. I'm sure that it will all work out, but right now, it's definitely one day at a time."

CASE HISTORY   Phil A.

Phil A. is an experienced county personnel supervisor. He sums up his perception of the many employees he has seen retire throughout his career.

"The first month or so after you retire the reality hasn't sunk in that you're never going back to work again; it just feels like a month's vacation. But then you wake up one morning and realize that you're not going back. You spend a greater proportion of your life in your work setting than you do with your family, and it's a major adjustment to suddenly give up something that you'd grown so totally acclimated to.

"It's like when you were single and had a bunch of guys you ran around with, and then one of the guys got married. He was no longer a member of the group, an outcast. That's just like what the retiree feels — he's an outcast, and he doesn't know how to get back in. He doesn't fit in any longer with the guys still working because he can't talk about the day-to-day things. His networks are all gone. The only things he can talk about are the things that happened in the past.

"Some retirees open a small business or try to create a new career. One guy bought an orchard and spends all his time taking care of his trees. He's still making money, being productive, *doing something*.

"Most workers take things on a day-to-day basis, and think of retirement as a far-away and abstract concept. Then, all of a sudden, the day comes. They haven't prepared for all the idle time. Maybe they spent the first month or two fixing up the house, but when the house and yard are all fixed up, then what? Lots of guys say, 'I'm going to play golf every day.' It seldom works out that way. Who are they going to play with three or four times a week? Most people are still out there making a living, and don't have time.

"There are more than a few retirees who don't make a good adjustment, and who stay lost. They can't seem to take control of their lives and get into something new. I think this is usually the result of not really planning for retirement."

Retirement for Today's Mid-life Workers

In contrast to past generations, today's mid-life worker may find his or her eventual retirement much less comfortable. Today's workers are much more mobile, and are not as likely to spend their entire career with the same organization as workers have in the past. Corporate restructuring, plant shutdowns, changing technology and shifting markets have dramatically affected the length of time people stay at the same job. This directly affects funding a pension, and can easily nullify the ability to qualify for pension benefits.

Related to frequent job switching is the fact that many younger workers cash out their pension funds early. According to one report, four out of five receive lump sum settlements and spend the proceeds rather than putting them in individual retirement accounts. According to the Department of Labor, workers who switched jobs collected approximately $12 billion in early retirement savings. Yet, despite having to pay accumulated taxes and a 10 percent penalty, those same workers managed to spend $9.6 billion of that money on automobiles and consumer goods! While this might have enhanced their standard of living in the short run, the long-term implications for their retirement are startling and frightening.

The Baby Boomers, who will begin to retire shortly after the year 2000, tend to live on the financial edge. They carry more debt than equity, and, as a result, have a thin cushion for the transition into retirement. In 1989, these consumers tapped into nearly $95 billion of the equity in their homes, and increased their debt-to-asset ratio by nearly 30 percent. The economics of this lifestyle are not compatible with the way our society structures retirement. Comfortable retirement is based on the assumption of being debt-free and independently secure.

The Baby Boomers, who will begin to retire shortly after the year 2000, tend to live on the financial edge. They carry more debt than equity, and, as a result, have a thin cushion for the transition into retirement.

Recently, as a consequence of the junk bond crisis, some pension funds have been seriously undermined. Thousands of workers now face the reality of never being able to collect their pension benefits, even though they may have paid into the funds for years or decades.

Facing the Reality of Living — and Dying

Preparing ourselves for the later years of life is essential. The "Golden Years" are filled with challenges and transitions. Illness and associated medical expenses must be anticipated. The death of lifelong friends, including life partners, becomes a persistent and disturbing reality. Major financial adjustments are likely to be necessary. And adjusting to a totally different lifestyle can be traumatic indeed.

Preparing ourselves for the later years of life is essential. Major financial adjustments are likely to be necessary, and adjusting to a totally different lifestyle can be traumatic indeed.

Building a support system of friends and family is essential, as is planning ahead and being realistic about what might occur. It is important to have a will and anticipate the needs of surviving spouses and family members. Making funeral arrangements in advance might seem morbid to some, but it is actually liberating (and a very thoughtful thing to do for surviving family members). Knowing that we have done all we can regarding our final care is a very healthy way of facing the reality of our own mortality. A healthy attitude is exhibited by the snappy come-back line from a retiree who is asked how he's feeling: "I have good days and bad days, and that's all right, considering the alternative!"

All aspects of retirement life should be openly discussed with those affected by major decisions (family members and close friends). Most of the psychological stressors associated with our later years can be significantly alleviated if a pragmatic and intelligent plan is developed, shared and put into effect prior to retirement.

Making a Healthy Transition into Retirement

The following suggestions are derived directly from psychotherapeutic work with individuals going through the retirement process:

Life is always moving forward. Learn to live in the present. Remaining "stuck" in the past only leads to depression or frustration.

MAINTAIN a positive survival spirit. Remember that life is always moving forward. Learn to live in the present. Remaining "stuck" in the past only leads to depression or frustration. Share positive thoughts and actions with others to create an environment of active and productive energy.

LIMIT major lifestyle changes for a specific period of time — six months to a year. Major life changes always create stress, and time should be allowed for any necessary adjustments. Setting realistic short-term goals helps us achieve our objectives while still enjoying a sense of well-being.

AVOID a "poor me" attitude — forego self pity! It's self-defeating to complain. Besides, friends and relatives will get tired of hearing it and stay away.

REEVALUATE! Retirement does not mean forced idleness. For compulsive, Type A personalities, not working can be traumatic. Compulsive work patterns are often a sign of running away from personal psychological issues or deeper emotional conflicts. Retirement can be a time to reflect on our past reasons for working so hard. Learning to do nothing, or at least learning to do much less, is actually doing something! Look upon retirement as providing a time to reflect, relax and formulate new plans for life.

PLAN systematically and flexibly. Don't get "stuck" in one mode. Remember, we make our own schedules and plans, and we can change them if we want to. Our only real obligations are the ones we choose!

LEARN to cope with feelings of loss of control and power, and recognize that they're not really well-founded. During our working years, we grow accustomed to having some sense of control over our life and destiny, and we worry that retirement will lead to the loss of that control. Not true. Retirement can actually provide more freedom than we ever had before. Amazingly, the idea of freedom is petrifying for those who would rather avoid the challenge of developing a meaning and purpose for each and every day.

The idea of freedom is petrifying for those who would rather avoid the challenge of developing a meaning and purpose for each and every day.

ADJUST financial requirements. Retirement generally means reduced income, and it's our responsibility to study our financial position in detail and make necessary adjustments. Having a clear understanding of personal finances can greatly reduce stress and frustration.

DEVELOP new ways of coping, especially if a spouse is still working. Remember that our retirement is our own, and we must find our own meaning and purpose in life. A partner has his or her own agenda, and we have ours. When a husband who has been the primary breadwinner retires, it is not the wife's responsibility to provide a new purpose or direction for him. Nor should she have to make major changes in her routine and habits to fit in with the new situation. Open communication between partners is essential to facilitate a smooth transition into retirement.

FIND new interests or hobbies, or reestablish old ones. The most devastating and self-defeating approach to retirement is to treat it as simply "killing time." We must remember that life is, in its simplest terms, just time; if we kill time, we are killing a part of life we can never recapture.

DEVOTE time to community, spiritual or other endeavors. This interaction with others promotes a contemporary mindset, and also represents a way to give something back to the community. Socializing also counteracts feelings that may arise from self-pity or fantasies about the way things used to be.

Retirement is a normal and expected phase of life. The retirement years can, and should be, just as productive, active and exciting as all the previous years combined.

Retirement is not the end of the "Book of Life," but just another chapter. Retirement signifies only the cessation of work, and we must see it as a normal and expected phase of life. The retirement years can, and should be, just as productive, active and exciting as all the previous years combined. This excitement just takes a different shape. There are countless examples of public figures who have maintained their creativity and vitality, and who have contributed to and participated in community and world affairs. These role models can teach us something about successful retirement, and serve as a foundation for our own retirement years.

SUMMARY — CHAPTER SIX

Stress on retirees
- ≡ Isolation from families or others in the community
- ≡ Boredom and lack of meaning and purpose
- ≡ Financial problems
- ≡ Health problems
- ≡ Health care costs

Stress on future retirees
- ≡ Pensions depleted by current layoffs, job-changing and corporate failures
- ≡ Lack of savings — Baby Boomers live on the financial edge.

Solutions
- ≡ Plan ahead for retirement.
- ≡ Maintain a positive survival spirit — don't get stuck in the past.
- ≡ Initially limit major lifestyle changes.
- ≡ Build a support system of friends and family.
- ≡ Avoid self pity.
- ≡ Reevaluate lifelong attitudes; learn new ways to cope.
- ≡ Adjust financial requirements.
- ≡ Develop new interests and hobbies.
- ≡ Socialize; devote time to community and spiritual concerns.

Chapter Seven

The Human Burnout Syndrome — When and How It Began

"Stop the world, I want to get off!" is a comic expression that, while it may make us laugh, has an underlying truthfulness. For many, life seems too fast and too hectic.

Sometimes, the confusion around us is so great that we cannot discriminate between the important *signals* that we need to deal with and the *noise* that distracts us. Signals give us essential information about our real needs, while noise and distractions waste our energy and prevent us from staying in touch with who we are and what we want out of life. All too often, we find ourselves overwhelmed by the demanding signals and noise in our environment, and react by withdrawing or fantasizing about living a carefree existence, perhaps on a tropical island in the middle of nowhere.

Time Consciousness and the Origins of Stress

Life in America wasn't always so hectic. While conditions may have been more harsh for past generations, life was also less complicated. America began as a predominantly agricultural country, and the last two centuries have seen a gradual, yet increasingly distinct, separation between rural and urban societies and a marked decline in the percentage of the population engaged in agriculture. A key event in this process occurred approximately 150 years ago with the coming of the railroad, thus accelerating the pace of urban population growth. This, in turn, required the transportation of ever-increasing quantities of food and commodities from rural to urban areas. The gradual criss-crossing of the country by rail-road lines and the always-present telegraph wires linked the whole country together as never before.

The expanding transportation system required sophisti-cated scheduling, and Americans began to learn to operate within specific time frames. They learned the meaning of the word *deadline*. For American farmers, there was a fundamental shift from raising crops primarily to feed their own families to raising crops to sell at the market. The watch and clock, previously considered luxury items, became necessities. "Time" was transformed from an abstract concept to a con-crete operating principle of life. Americans became time-con-scious and time-dependent. Instead of having control of their time, time began the insidious process of controlling them.

However, if we ask whether burnout really existed in the early years of the twentieth century, the answer is probably no. The Industrial Revolution benefited Americans in many respects; essential needs were being satisfied and material goods were available much more abundantly than they had ever been before. And, for the most part, workers were di-rectly participating in the process.

As the Industrial Revolution progressed, however, the pace accelerated even further. The telegraph and telephone became mandatory tools for the prosperous business and a status symbol in the home. Instant communications — with the implication that orders had to be delivered on time and deadlines had to be met — became the norm. Electrification allowed factories to flourish and produce goods around the clock. The assembly line never stopped. The image of Charlie

During the Industrial Revolution, "time" was transformed from an abstract concept to a concrete operating principle of life. However, if we ask whether burnout really existed in the early years of the twentieth century, the answer is probably no.

Chaplin trying to keep up with the line in the movie *Modern Times* symbolized the plight of the American factory worker as the Industrial Revolution roared along.

The advent of transcontinental air travel in the 1920s, although it was initially used only by the privileged few, forged a relatively rapid path between the East and West coasts — not to mention linking America with Europe and Asia — and set the stage for the concept of a "global village." The interstate highway system, begun in the 1950s, made long-distance auto travel commonplace, and allowed the American population to become even more mobile. These dynamics created a world of instant communication — and demands from all directions had to be met at an ever-increasing pace.

The Impact of Twenty-first Century Communication

There has never been a time in history when communication networks have been more multifaceted, immediate and demanding as they are today. Modern communications systems involve ever-greater volumes of data transferred at tremendous, even instantaneous, speeds through ever-increasing channels.

Traditionally, communication consisted of speaking, writing or reading. There was time to assimilate and analyze information being received; time to digest what it meant and make rational decisions based on that analysis. People had time to "decompress." *No more!*

The typical American today is bombarded with information from radio, cable television, movies, billboards, computer bulletin boards and fax messages. And they're always urgent.

Just one example: In the business world of the 1950s, a cross-country telephone call and confirming letter via first-class mail was considered state of the art. By the 1980s, overnight express was the cutting edge. In the 1990s, fax messages

There has never been a time in history when communication networks have been more multifaceted, immediate and demanding as they are today. Modern communications systems involve ever-greater volumes of data transferred at tremendous, even instantaneous, speeds through ever-increasing channels.

zip back and forth across the continents, the global financial markets operate day and night and satellite computer networks allow subscribers to conduct "real-time" on-line communication all over the world.

The net effect of all these new technologies is to speed up the pace of human interaction and create constant demands for instantaneous response. People *must* respond, and respond *immediately*, when information is received. We begin to feel that we have no choice in the matter, that we absolutely must respond to whatever data stimulus we receive, and that we have to do it *right now!*

The technological revolution has evolved into the Information Age. The transmission and processing of information are now the primary activities of our society and business world. We produce less and communicate more. We rely less on the physical, and more on the abstract parts of life. The result is often stimulus overload, a frenzied condition that places unrealistic and frequently absurd demands on us. The consequences, as we shall see, can be devastating.

The transmission and processing of information are now the primary activities of our society and business world. The result is often stimulus overload, a frenzied condition that imposes unrealistic and frequently absurd demands on us.

Moving Beyond Denial

Each of us, at least to some degree, is mired in a state of denial — denial of who we are and what we really want out of life. Denial makes it impossible to accurately define our own situation or "see the forest for the trees." One consequence of chronic denial is that we tend to bend over backwards to justify our actions; we want to believe that what we're doing is just exactly what we're supposed to be doing. We move forward with our blinders on, treating any deviation from our preconceived notion of what life is all about with irrational fear. Even worse, rather than dealing with those fears, we avoid them, holding ourselves psychologically captive in a futile attempt to maintain our comfort or safety zone. The inevitable result is that self-exploration and personal development are sacrificed in an effort to maintain our own psychological and emotional stability.

Denial also generates a vague sense of anxiety and lack of fulfillment — it's all too easy to blame our conflicted emotions on someone or something else. Each of us finds different scapegoats, with work, family life and early childhood upbringing all being likely suspects.

This pervasive *blaming* of external factors often leads us to seek solutions from outside ourselves as well. For many, this takes the form of the friendly therapist who puts us in touch with our abused "inner child." However, while it is true that there are many who have had troubled early lives, which we generally blame on growing up in a dysfunctional family, we're not being fair to ourselves if we use that as an excuse for our problems in adult life. Sadly, there is often a conspiracy of common interest between client and therapist to focus on the past and blame others for the client's current unhappiness and inadequate coping processes.

Others seek solace in multi-step programs, using them as collective safety nets into which they dump their emotional refuse. Compulsive disorders are essentially replaced by compulsive dependency, and many find themselves on a never-ending merry-go-round, pursuing the elusive (and unattainable) goal of total normalcy.

Whatever the specific form taken by the outside "crutch," overreliance on others reinforces our own fears and, especially, our feelings of inadequacy. Compulsive dependency creates a massive barrier to confronting and taking responsibility for our own life situation, emotional needs and expectations. Until there is a realization that there is no "magic key" to happiness, and that each of us is ultimately responsible for our own mental health, this same sad cycle will be repeated.

Denial generates a vague sense of anxiety and lack of fulfillment — it's all too easy to blame our conflicted emotions on someone or something else.

SUMMARY — CHAPTER SEVEN

The history of burnout

≡ Urban growth and separation of rural and urban societies began with the advent of railroad transportation approximately 150 years ago.

≡ The Industrial Revolution — and the assembly line — accelerated the pace.

≡ Telephones and telegraphs made communication instantaneous.

≡ Transcontinental air travel also allowed businesses to expand their operations.

≡ Deadlines became important; Americans became time-conscious and time-dependent.

≡ Today, computers, faxes and satellite systems speed up human interaction and create constant demands for quick response.

≡ The world has become a "global village."

Burnout and denial

≡ Chronic denial clouds the issues and prevents their resolution.

≡ Denial creates a necessity for the burnout sufferer to "bend over backwards" to justify his actions.

≡ Denial generates a vague sense of anxiety and lack of fulfillment.

≡ Denial fosters a tendency to blame others.

≡ For some, multi-step programs can function as collective safety nets, replacing compulsive disorders with compulsive dependency.

Chapter Eight

Stress, Anxiety and Depression — The Early Stages of Burnout

Man's greatest triumph is victory over himself —
his weaknesses, fears and anxieties.
— *Gerald Loren Fishkin*

The Three Stages of Stress

Burnout has its roots in stress, which may be defined as *any demand — internal, external or both — that forces a person to mentally and physically readjust in an effort to maintain a sense of balance in life.*

At the most basic level, the psychological consequences of stress depend upon the ways we have learned to cope with difficulties throughout our life. Specific bodily and emotional responses are triggered by the way we perceive signals in our environment. Our personality is the critical variable that determines our reaction to stressors — the more stable our personality, the better we will be able to cope with constant exposure to external demands.

In reality, of course, we all experience stress on a daily basis; even the ordinary demands and pressures of mundane events, and especially our own thoughts, generate a certain amount of tension. In fact, stress is also an integral part of the

We all experience stress on a daily basis; even the ordinary demands and pressures of mundane events, and especially our own thoughts, generate a certain amount of tension.

competitive spirit, setting and achieving goals and the ebb and flow of interpersonal relationships. We have to understand that stressors exist all around us, and this is neither a good nor a bad situation. The key is how productively — or counter-productively — we deal with the demands placed on us by others and, even more importantly, the demands we place on ourselves.

When the stressors associated with daily life become over-whelming, and our previously effective coping processes are no longer effective in dealing with them, our internal or automatic defense systems begin to break down. The resulting emotional pain can reach overwhelming proportions. At this point, somehow, modifications must be made in the way we think, act and react. If such modifications are not made, *we are headed for burnout!*

In dealing with any personal difficulty, whether it's interpersonal conflict, marital problems or alcohol/drug abuse, we employ automatic, learned coping mechanisms in an effort to readjust to changing demands. What we're really trying to do is to establish a state of psychological, emotional and social balance. While each of us has a deeply ingrained need to maintain a personal sense of control over our life situation, the coping mechanisms we have developed over the years may or may not be well suited for dealing with a particular stressor. When we attempt to bring a stressor under control, but lack appropriate, positive coping mechanisms, the likely result is an even further escalation of stress.

Stress and the General Adaptation Syndrome

We owe much of our understanding of stress to Dr. Hans Selye, who devoted most of his professional career to the clinical exploration of the causes and consequences of stress.

Particularly valuable to our understanding of stress is his three-phase model of stress coping known as the General Adaptation Syndrome (GAS). Popularly referred to as the *fight-or-flight* syndrome, it has three phases:

The Alarm Stage

When we initially become aware of a specific signal requiring a response, our bodies begin to secrete adrenaline. This "adrenaline pump" reaction instantaneously creates an adrenal rush that can be compared to the stimulating effects of coffee, nicotine or amphetamines.

However, the down side of the "high" deriving from this adrenaline discharge in the bloodstream is the chemical depression that frequently follows. Constant exposure to a stressor, with long periods spent in the alarm stage, may lead to exhaustion and physical deterioration. As adrenaline pumps into the body, it sends a signal, generally referred to as the *fight* stage of stress, that a perceived stressor must be warded off. Chemical changes also take place that eventually cause body tissue to break down. The cumulative results of prolonged stress can range from simple headaches to more serious ailments such as ulcers, cardiovascular and neuromuscular disorders and various other physical and mental conditions.

The cumulative results of prolonged stress can range from simple headaches to more serious ailments such as ulcers, cardiovascular and neuromuscular disorders and various other physical and mental conditions.

The Resistance Stage

During this stage, we attempt to employ our learned mental and physical responses to "learn to live with" the stressor. As soon as we identify the stressor as representing a probable threat, learned psychological and physical defense mechanisms (referred to as coping mechanisms) come into play to quell or attempt to neutralize the stressor. While much of this process may occur beneath our level of conscious awareness, it represents the second phase of coping with stress.

During the stages of alarm (fight) and resistance (flight), as we attempt to adjust to the internal pressures of a stressor, we often experience the emotions of anxiety, depression, low frustration tolerance and hostility. The discharge of adrenaline can lead to a nasty "emotional roller coaster" effect. Ultimately, the hostility and rage created by the tension must be effectively vented if we are to return to a state of equilibrium or balance.

Selye found that repeated exposure to a noxious agent or stressor weakens our acquired defenses, as well as the immune system, ultimately rendering us ineffective in combating stress. Since adrenaline continues to circulate throughout the body during the Resistance stage, to be effective, our defense mechanisms (behaviors) must both combat the stressor and turn off the adrenal (alarm) responses. If our response is not effective in turning off the alarm, we enter the third stage — exhaustion. (However, if our coping behavior is effective, the exhaustion stage is effectively bypassed.)

Repeated exposure to a noxious agent or stressor weakens our acquired defenses, as well as the immune system, ultimately rendering us ineffective in combating stress.

The Exhaustion Stage

When attempts to cope with the stressor are ineffective, and stress becomes cumulative, over a period of time psychological and physical exhaustion sets in. Ultimately, the final state of complete exhaustion is death. However, the relevant point here is that the onset of the exhaustion stage corresponds to what we refer to as burnout. If we reach the exhaustion stage, we are totally unable to maintain a sense of personal equilibrium. The ineffectiveness of our previously learned methods of coping render our efforts to deal with the outside stressor ineffective also. At this point, we move beyond simple stress and become, essentially, dysfunctional. Burnout affects all aspects of our existence, including the physical, psychological, social and emotional dimensions.

CASE HISTORY   Stephen J.

When the Healer Needs Healing

Stephen J., a 38-year-old emergency room physician, sought counseling for what he characterized as "some problems" he had been experiencing over a period of months. This case illustrates the way in which pre-existing personality characteristics can predispose us to depression. It also shows how depression can be overcome. In this case, early detection and treatment resulted in a complete remission of symptoms after one year of intensive, individual psychotherapy.

"I was so stressed out about my working conditions that it's hard to put into words. I worked 65 to 80 hours a week, and there were simply not enough hours in the day. I couldn't seem to leave my work behind when I left the hospital each day.

"To compensate for my absence from home, my wife went on spending sprees to make sure we 'kept up' with the other doctors and their wives. I had to work even harder to pay the bills. Our kids had no sense of reality; they got the material goods they wanted, but not enough love and 'quality time.' We were a mechanical family. We made all the motions, but there was no soul.

"I suffered a 40-pound weight loss, always had insomnia, couldn't concentrate, make decisions...I was a wreck. I got to where I didn't even care about my recreational activities, which had always been centrally important to me. I used to play golf, ski, hunt and coach Little League baseball and foot-

ball. But I just lost interest. I was smoking two packs a day and drinking a lot of alcohol so I could sleep. I didn't want to burden my wife with my work problems, and just 'clammed up' when she asked what was wrong. This just made our marital problems worse. I was so tense, I even had extramarital affairs to relieve the tension. Fortunately, I kept them segregated from my family life and they left no permanent damage. I got so desperate that I was willing to sacrifice the best parts of my life with my family.

"I later realized that my depression resulted from my anger about everything. I was trapped in a situation where I felt I had no control over my life. Since I've been getting help, I've learned how to monitor my stress levels. I'm also learning to acknowledge my anger and to express my inner feelings. This helps me deal with the stress that continues in my work, and makes it much easier to maintain a healthy family life."

Psychological Aspects of Stress

The effects of stress on the human body can be compared to the demands for electrical current a car makes on its battery. If the energy emitted by the battery to provide power is not replenished effectively and consistently — that is, if the battery does not recharge itself — the result will be a depleted, and ultimately dead, battery. For humans, energy-depleting demands come from many sources:

- o The need for recognition
- o Demands/expectations of our occupations or professional roles
- o Demands/expectations of our social roles
- o Dealing with individual and family problems and crises
- o Dealing with authority
- o The lack of communication regarding emotional issues

Symptoms of Cumulative or Excessive Stress

We all react differently to stress. Even though hundreds of individuals might be exposed to the same stress-provoking situation — say, the loss of a job — each of them is likely to cope with it differently. Those with a sense of adequacy, competence and self-worth might be able to better cope with a similar stressful situation than those who perceive the situation as life-threatening or catastrophic.

Analysis of hundreds of case histories has led to the identification of a number of symptoms caused by stress. The following are only a representative sampling of the effects of cumulative stress:

Those with a sense of adequacy, competence and self-worth might be able to better cope than those who perceive a similar stressful situation as life-threatening or catastrophic.

Symptoms of Stress

- Excessive weight gain or loss in a short period of time
- Combativeness, irritability, impulsiveness, hostility
- An exaggerated sense of despair
- Excessive use of sick leave (often related to alcoholism and chronic fatigue); job-related injuries
- Frequent use of alcohol or mood-altering drugs
- Marital and family conflict
- Sexual dysfunction
- Inappropriate display of emotions when a more rational or calm approach would be appropriate
- Exaggerated fears about health or job-related injury
- Physical distress, e.g., stomach problems, heart disease, hyperventilation, low back pain, non-specific musculo-skeletal pain, diabetes
- Frequent complaints regarding personal finances
- Verbalized feelings of isolation and/or alienation from others ("Nobody understands me!")
- Overcompensating and arrogant behavior
- Personality breakdown, frequent crying jags
- Loss of interest in work, family, hobbies
- Increased number of accidents, including vehicular or other types that may cause physical injury
- Acute or chronic fatigue
- Insomnia, including nightmares and stressful dreams
- Alteration of "normal" work patterns and habits

Anticipating Distress — Our Ever-present Anxiety

One of the primary factors that distinguishes humans from other species is that our behavior is ruled by intellect rather than pure instinct. However, another distinction, one that is

One of the primary factors that distinguishes humans from other species is that our behavior is ruled by intellect rather than pure instinct.

more relevant to our discussion of burnout, is that we are likely to respond to distressing situations by experiencing anxiety. This can be contrasted with the reaction of fear exhibited by animals lower on the phylogenetic scale.

However, anxiety should not be confused with the emotional response of fear. Although both anxiety and fear are associated with some of the same physical sensations, they represent two distinctly different emotional states.

Fear is a brief emotional state in response to a real danger that is consciously identified and understood. Once the danger is identified, hopefully, a proper response is generated. Eventually, the danger signal either passes or is overcome. At that point, the emotional reaction of fear subsides.

In contrast, anxiety has an intangible and long-lasting effect that may linger indefinitely. Vague feelings of mental and emotional discomfort invade the mind, seemingly from all directions at once, and the effect may be a paralysis of the senses and a resulting inability to respond effectively. Anxiety is sometimes called "psychic pain," and those who have experienced it know how apt this description really is.

Typical Reactions Associated with Anxiety

Motor and Muscular Tension
This usually takes the form of shaking, jumpiness, trembling, tensed-up muscles and an inability to relax.

Autonomic Nervous System Hyperactivity
Excessive perspiration, heart palpitations, dry mouth, dizziness, and frequent urination.

Gastrointestinal Symptoms
Diarrhea, stomach upset and digestive problems are common.

Extreme Apprehension

The person suffering from anxiety is frequently plagued with feelings of mental discomfort and worry. All thoughts are likely to be negative, with overwhelming feelings that "Something terrible is about to happen!"

Hyper-vigilance

There is often a persistent "uptight" feeling. The victim of anxiety is often impatient, irritable and ready to explode at the slightest stimulus. At the same time, it is hard to concentrate and difficult or impossible to get a good night's sleep.

The degree of anxiety we experience is heavily influenced by the way in which we perceive the threat that confronts us. Most centrally, our level of anxiety depends on how we assess the threat's potential consequences to our own sense of well-being. The effects of anxiety can perhaps be better understood in light of chemical processes that take place within the body, particularly the role played by the hormone adrenaline. A state of anxiety stimulates the body, and, in so doing, also stimulates the adrenal gland's production of adrenaline. When this powerful hormone is released into the bloodstream, the resulting condition is Selye's fight-or-flight syndrome. All of us can recall times when we've gone into this state, perhaps in a "near miss" while driving. The discharge of adrenaline leads to increased heart and respiratory rates, sweating, constriction of blood vessels and dilated pupils.

Exposure to high levels of adrenaline discharged over a period of time can be quite destructive. Reflexes tighten, we become immobilized and our reactions slow down. But how do we know when we're experiencing too much anxiety — and how do we know when it's really harming us?

The person suffering from anxiety is frequently plagued with feelings of mental discomfort and worry. All thoughts are likely to be negative.

Exposure to high levels of adrenaline discharged over a period of time can be quite destructive. Sustained anxiety can, and often does, lead to the breakdown of body tissue.

Whenever an event, person or threat that triggers our anxiety response becomes the focal point of our life, the result is internal conflict and the disruption of normal thought processes. This in turn leads to disruptive behavior patterns and, sometimes, even physical illness. Sustained anxiety can, and often does, lead to the breakdown of body tissue. Some of the possible physical effects are ulcers, headaches, fatigue, heart disease, stroke and diabetes. Clinical observations also suggest that chronic anxiety is also related to back pain and gastrointestinal disorders.

Anxiety can also result from psychological defense mechanisms that automatically or subconsciously protect us from dealing with unacceptable thoughts or impulses. Perhaps we have an overwhelming urge to tell off the boss, express our anger or frustration to a close friend or pick a fight with the obnoxious teenager sitting behind us at a movie. We are socialized to believe that these impulses are antisocial and that they should not be acted upon. As a result, our subconscious mind represses these impulses and keeps us from actually doing what we feel like doing. However — and this is the negative part — this suppression or repression of our impulses also triggers frustration and anxiety.

The implication is that individuals who maintain very rigid modes of thinking and being, who repress most of their impulses, may experience excessive anxiety. This anxiety results from the denial of basic thoughts and feelings. The result: a loss of self-knowledge and emotional isolation. For many, the constant need to maintain emotional distance blocks the communication of feelings and heightens personal anxiety.

Ironically, we seldom directly confront the real stressors in our life (that is, the actual source of our anxiety). Instead, we attempt to cope, and the negative physical and mental arousal this causes only contributes to the burnout process.

Excessive levels of anxiety result in a heightened sense of internal pressure. If this pressure is not relieved, the inevitable result is a negative impact on our overall behavior — especially within our family, social and occupational roles.

Anxiety and Compulsive Disorders

Dealing with anxiety is never easy, and trying to cope with anxiety incorrectly only makes matters worse. For many of us, compulsive behaviors represent futile attempts to control our emotions by external actions. But this is inside out, and just doesn't work! Instead, we need to understand and deal with our anxiety and other emotions in a healthy manner, regardless of how difficult this may be at first.

Constantly trying to deal with the emotions generated by anxiety can lead to the development of what mental health workers refer to as "compulsive disorders." Most of us, however, refer to them simply as "addictions." These addictions often take such forms as:

- Excessive eating, frequent bingeing
- Workaholism
- Compulsive shopping (shopaholic)
- Compulsive sexual behavior (sexaholic)
- Excessive use of power or authority (power freak)

Excessive Eating/Bingeing

Obviously, we all must eat to survive — if we don't eat, we die. However, since most of us don't have to worry about starvation, eating often serves other needs. Beyond simple sustenance, the motivation for eating has more to do with what eating represents to us, and this may cause us to use it (or misuse it) to cope with anxiety. If we are frustrated, bored or emotionally isolated from the world — in short, experi-

Eating often serves other needs. We may turn to food as a way of satisfying our psychological needs or feelings of emotional emptiness.

encing anxiety — we may turn to food as a way of satisfying our psychological needs or feelings of emotional emptiness. Eating can represent a way of filling ourselves up or a "reward" in a life that offers little in the way of outside appreciation. In short, it can be an attempt to counteract the painful emotions of feeling detached, empty and alone. However, satisfaction from this source is short-lived and does nothing to address the basis of the anxiety. Unfortunately, even though the "satisfaction" may be quite short-lived, the excess body tissue remains as a testimonial that something is wrong!

Compulsive Work Patterns (Workaholic)

Compulsive behaviors or disorders do not add to any insight or knowledge about the underlying source of our unhappiness.

Most Americans work outside the home, spending one third or more of their lives at their place of employment. When confronted with anxiety, too many of us throw ourselves into our work with a vengeance. We use compulsive work behavior to avoid dealing with anxiety (or any other emotion, for that matter). Just as with other compulsive behaviors or disorders, however, this does not add to any insight or knowledge about the underlying source of our unhappiness. Instead, it often makes the situation worse and may contribute to the deterioration of personal and family life.

Excessive Spending (Shopaholic)

The spending of money has many meanings, and most of them have nothing to do with buying food for the family or making the mortgage payment. Money represents power and control, and some of us react to anxiety and distress by going on spending sprees. The average American has a wallet full of credit cards, and it's pretty easy to spend beyond our means. Maintaining a high debt-to-income ratio can, and often does, have the effect of keeping us constantly concerned about money (or the lack of money), resulting in an ongoing distraction from any deeper-level emotional issues.

Compulsive Sexual Behavior (Sexaholic)

Sexual relations with our partner can be among the most gratifying of all our activities, providing a means for attaining a sense of fulfillment and pleasure. The most mature form of sexual interaction is expressed in the sharing of a mutually pleasurable act while enhancing a relationship. However, the person faced with excessive anxiety may instead engage in increased sexual activity purely as a means of discharging internal pressures. Sex of this type is likely to be compulsive, and may be no more than a "performance." Under these circumstances:

The most mature form of sexual interaction is the sharing of a mutually pleasurable act while enhancing a relationship. However, the anxiety victim may use it as a means of discharging internal pressures.

- ° There is little or no concern for the other person, who is perceived as an "object" existing solely for gratification.
- ° Sexual conquest functions as a measure of self-worth or self-esteem.
- ° Sexual behavior is a substitute for other needs that are not being satisfied in a healthy, mature way.

A high level of anxiety can also lead to sexual dysfunction. Among men, problems include the inability to respond to sexual stimulation, impotence, the inability to maintain an erection and premature ejaculation. For women, excessive anxiety may result in a lowering or loss of sex drive or painful intercourse due to insufficient genital lubrication.

Excessive Discretionary Use of Power (Power Freak)

Some of us may work out our frustrations by exercising an autocratic and dictatorial style in dealing with others. While this type of behavior is most common in the workplace, it may also be exhibited on the home front. While treating others in an aggressive or heavy-handed way may relieve our underlying frustrations and tensions in the short-term, it also reinforces the belief that we must remain in control at all costs and at all times.

The Many Faces of Depression

A lot of what we see in our society is a malaise that we call deep despair and depression. Rather than teaching each other to adapt to what we have, it would be better to honor the despair and allow a person to be in that despair until he comes through it, hopefully in a more evolved fashion, if he's got support for it.

— *Ram Das*

Most of us have experienced depression at some point in our lives, usually during the active phase of a life crisis. It may have ranged from a mild sadness to more severe depression. Hopefully, we learned from our experience, recovered with only a few emotional scars and gained new insights about who we are in the process.

A poor self-image and a perceived lack of control contribute to a downward mental and emotional spiral of despair and, ultimately, depression.

For some, however, the combination of life's calamities, a poor self-image and a perceived lack of control contribute to a downward mental and emotional spiral of despair and, ultimately, depression. Anyone who has ever been affected by such depression knows that the road back is painful and difficult.

We cannot survive the constant depletion of our psychological and physical resources without harm to our body. There has been considerable interest in recent years in evaluating the effects of sustained exposure to stressors; considerable research has led to the identification of the Epstein-Barr virus. This has also been associated with "Chronic Fatigue Syndrome," sometimes referred to as the "Yuppie Flu" because of its tendency to strike ambitious, overachieving individuals.

The primary signs and symptoms of Chronic Fatigue Syndrome are:
- Fatigue
- Depression
- Difficulty expressing ideas
- Swelling of lymph nodes
- Pain in the joints
- Headache, dizziness and abnormal sensations without apparent cause
- Sore throat/low grade fever
- Chest pain/heart palpitation
- Upper respiratory distress
- Gastrointestinal disorders

Depression is not the result of any single element or experience. Instead, it results from the complex interaction of our genetic and biological make-up, our early life experiences and role models, our unique way of perceiving the world and processing information and our methods of handling stress and frustration.

The Symptoms of Depression

There are certain symptoms that are typical of depression. Depressed individuals are often not aware of the emotional changes that are taking place, even though their families, friends and co-workers can clearly observe the destructive aspects of depression. We need to recognize and understand the symptoms of depression, which include:

Depressed individuals are often not aware of the emotional changes that are taking place, even though others can clearly observe the destructive aspects of depression.

Dysphoric Mood
An all-pervasive sense of doom and gloom, often described

as a "sinking experience" or "internal death." As this mood takes hold, the emotional pain can become so great that there is a complete loss of interest in previously gratifying hobbies, sports activities and other previously rewarding pastimes.

Social Withdrawal

Loss of pleasure and meaning in life have a profound effect on the depressed individual. The basic instinct is to crawl into a cocoon to seek protection from the outside world. The irony, of course, is that the isolation perpetuates the depression.

Anxiety, Fear and Heightened Concern about Physical Ailments

Anxiety associated with depression may cause changes in brain chemistry and contribute to psychomotor agitation, tremors, tenseness and irritability. When we are depressed, we harbor foreboding thoughts, and fearfully anticipate the unknown, especially physical illness. This compounds the other symptoms of depression.

When we are depressed, we harbor foreboding thoughts, and fearfully anticipate the unknown. This compounds the other symptoms of depression.

Psychomotor Retardation and Significantly Decreased Energy Levels

Neurochemical processes come into play here, with neurotransmitters such as norepinephrine and serotonin being absorbed by the brain. These biochemical substances have an effect similar to adrenaline. The overall process can be compared to an out-of-tune carburetor in a car that uses too much gas and takes in too little oxygen, so that the engine lacks the energy to do its job effectively and efficiently. Being depressed depletes our total energy system.

Appetite Changes

Depression can cause some to lose all interest in food. Others eat compulsively, not because they are hungry, but from a deep sense of frustration or anger that they cannot understand.

Sleep Disturbance

Insomnia is common, as are dreams filled with themes of self-condemnation and guilt. There is an inability to sleep soundly, and a tendency to wake up feeling fearful and shaky. Waking does not bring rejuvenation, only a sense of being just as tired as the night before.

Low Self-esteem and Self-worth

When we are depressed, our thought patterns are dominated by feelings of inadequacy and negative self-worth. This sense of worthlessness, helplessness and hopelessness, representing a distorted perception of reality, reinforces a negative belief system.

> *When we are depressed, our thought patterns are dominated by feelings of inadequacy and negative self-worth. This distorted perception of reality reinforces a negative belief system.*

Distortions of Thinking and Faulty Information Processing

As depression deepens, distorted thoughts can lead to an inability to mentally focus or engage in effective problem solving. Various cognitive or thought distortions common in depression include:

- o **Over-personalization** — relating to or feeling impacted by everything in the outside world, even if no logical connection truly exists
- o **Over-generalization** — always being on alert, waiting for the alarm, ever vigilant, waiting for a crisis or calamity to happen
- o **Bipolar thinking** — evaluating any situation or individual as either totally good or totally bad
- o **Misperception** — magnifying or minimizing the significance of particular events

Suicidal Ideation, Thoughts of Death or Suicidal Gesture

Thoughts of suicide and death symbolically represent a desperate need to escape the emotional pain and turmoil of depression. Death is seen as a release from the pervasive feelings of guilt, despair and loss of control.

Depression and Unvented Anger

Anger, whether about a particular source of frustration or a catastrophic life event such as the sudden loss of a loved one, may ultimately lead to a state of depression. When this occurs, and we can't seem to find a way to discharge that anger, we set ourselves up for depression in a big way. We have to recognize our anger in order to resolve it before depression takes over, sending us into a downward emotional spiral that can all too easily become burnout.

It might seem logical that depression will disappear after the immediate source of stress is alleviated. This is not necessarily true, particularly when there are other ongoing sources of stress.

It might seem logical that our depression will disappear after the immediate source of stress is alleviated. This is not necessarily true, particularly when there are other ongoing sources of stress in our lives. When the cumulative effects of stress result in impaired social and occupational functioning, the only appropriate course of action may be to remove ourselves from the stressful environment altogether.

Feelings of low self-worth can be triggered by physical problems such as a sudden disability that forces an individual to leave the work environment. Such events can bring about an emotional sense of loss which often triggers an episode of depression. This is especially common when we find ourselves suddenly unable to perform our normal work activities, and yet lack hobbies, interests or friends outside of the workplace to provide a balance. For most of us, our work role is the primary source of our identity and focus of our lives. Thus, it should not be surprising that the loss of a long-established *work* identity can distort our *personal* identity. This creates an overwhelming sense of despair, leaving us with no sense of meaning and purpose to our lives.

Self-medicating with Alcohol

Approximately 100 million Americans drink wine and spirits, many heavily. About one in 10 becomes an alcoholic. Most alcoholics are not the stereotypical down-and-out vagrants on skid row; in fact, fewer than five percent of American alcoholics fit this profile. Anyone can become an alcoholic — the mailman, a teacher, police officers, housewives — even someone in our own family.

According to the National Council on Alcoholism, approximately 10 percent of American workers suffer from alcoholism, costing their employers (conservatively) an additional 25 percent over and above their salaries. This includes losses due to absenteeism, reduced efficiency, on-the-job accidents and increased use of medical benefits.

It is essential that we understand the nature of alcoholism as it relates to stress and burnout. Alcoholism is a disease for which the cause is not clearly understood. Research has shown that some people have a genetic predisposition for alcoholism, and that certain childhood experiences also play a predisposing role. Abuse of alcohol can also be an effort to quell the effects of anxiety. However, this form of self-medication can be as destructive (or even more destructive) as the anxiety, stress or depression that precipitated the compulsive drinking behavior in the first place.

Regardless of its causes, however, alcoholism's consequences are clearly devastating. Early signs of alcoholism include memory blackouts, feelings of guilt and aggressive

It should not be surprising that the loss of a long-established work identity can distort our personal identity and create an overwhelming sense of despair.

Alcoholism's consequences are clearly devastating. Early signs of alcoholism include memory blackouts, feelings of guilt and aggressive behavior.

behavior. There is also an increasing tolerance to, and dependency on, alcohol. The alcoholic may appear to gain weight due to bloating. A flushed face and red eyes are common. Sexual desire may be reduced, and performance affected.

The effects of a hangover (e.g., excessive thirst, headache, fatigue, nausea and tremors) create a miserable post-drinking experience for the addicted drinker. At work, motivation suffers and tardiness and absenteeism increase. Slowed reflexes, especially distorted eye and hand coordination, often develop. A common response is to turn to self-medication, using aspirin, coffee and other stimulants in an effort to counteract chronic and overwhelming fatigue. When this fails, as it inevitably does, the alcoholic reverts to alcohol to dull the effects of anxiety.

The neurological effects of compulsive drinking include loss of recent and long-term memory, increased irritability and difficulties with abstract thinking.

Emotional and psychological effects include irritability, hostility, impulsiveness and demanding and cynical behavior. Frequent mood swings are common, reflecting the underlying depression and anxiety. The alcoholic finds it difficult to be objective or make healthy, self-affirming moral or ethical judgments. This latter tendency, naturally, contributes to the high incidence of marital and family problems among alcoholics.

The Alcoholic Personality

As was stated previously, alcoholics come from every walk of life, and each alcoholic has his or her own unique personality. However, there are certain personality features that are common among alcoholics.

If someone has a problem with alcohol, over a period of time, he or she loses self-confidence and avoids any self-directed or self-initiated behavior. The impaired self-concept of the alcoholic is then made even worse by feelings of being abandoned and isolated from society. This contributes to the tendency to seek out a supportive person on whom to depend, often a family member or a sympathetic employer. The bottom line is that the alcoholic's dependence on alcohol is accompanied by an emotional dependence on others. Most alcoholics seek out a co-dependent to validate their behavior.

Many alcoholics function emotionally at a level reflecting the age at which they became addicted to alcohol. This usually shows up when an alcoholic person is "acting out" frustrations; the specific behaviors demonstrated are generally reminiscent of the age at which the addiction first developed.

Despite the efforts to drown their emotions in alcohol, alcoholics are subject to recurrent anxiety attacks and mood swings. In the depths of the mood swing they experience strong emotions of depression and persistent, though vague, fears. Perhaps most fundamentally, the alcoholic does not take responsibility for his or her own behavior, instead seeking out scapegoats to blame for personal problems.

Marked personality changes often accompany the development of compulsive drinking. A quiet and shy person may suddenly exhibit aggressive behavior, while an outgoing person "closes down" and becomes reclusive. The alcoholic, feeling guilt and remorse, may engage in acting out behaviors ranging from violent bursts of anger to breakdowns and crying jags

The alcoholic may also become heavy-handed, acting in an authoritarian, non-supportive manner when a cooperative style would be much more appropriate. Frustrations and guilt may be acted out with loved ones, and even close friends are treated with hostility. Literally no one is spared the devastating consequences of alcohol use and abuse.

Over a period of time, the alcoholic loses self-confidence and avoids any self-directed or self-initiated behavior. Despite the efforts to drown their emotions in alcohol, alcoholics are subject to recurrent anxiety attacks and mood swings.

The acting out of unacceptable impulses forces the alcoholic to hide inner feelings of guilt, shame and remorse. Alcoholics constantly rationalize their drinking behavior, and bury their feelings of guilt and self-condemnation by taking yet another drink.

This acting out of unacceptable impulses forces the alcoholic to hide inner feelings of guilt, shame and remorse. Denial becomes the ultimate defense to preserve at least some remnants of self-esteem. Few alcoholics recognize their addiction for what it is, and most go out of their way to hide the implications of their drinking. Alcoholics constantly rationalize their drinking behavior, and bury their feelings of guilt and self-condemnation by taking yet another drink.

Alcoholics and Their Relationships

The alcoholic maintains emotional distance in interpersonal relationships, and often utilizes deceit and manipulation in interacting with others. The alcoholic may use drinking to desensitize an underlying distrust of others. The alcoholic also tends to avoid anyone who is disapproving, thus avoiding humiliation and rejection.

Family members, particularly the life partners of alcoholics, may be passive and emotionally dependent on the alcoholic. They are at substantial risk of becoming co-dependent. Fearful that confronting or attempting to change the abusive drinking would only create further disharmony, they give quiet or implied approval to the drinking excesses of their partners.

At some point, however, the alcoholic's spouse or significant other must refuse to continue to accept the behavior. Even though initial criticism is often met with violent outbursts and condemnation, this represents a major crossroad within their relationship. The alcoholic's anger must be seen for what it actually is — a cry for help. This is the point at which the alcoholic is most vulnerable, and it is up to the partner to demonstrate the resolve to establish a whole new set of ground rules for the relationship and treatment.

The Treatment of Alcoholism

Alcoholism is a disease that cannot really be cured. However, its destructiveness can be arrested and its victims restored to useful and productive lives.

Individual or group counseling is often sufficient to identify the warning signs and symptoms of chemical dependency. Such sessions provide a forum for mutual support in which chemically dependent individuals can discuss their abuse of alcohol or other drugs without fear of retribution. If the addiction cannot be controlled this way, the treatment of choice is generally detoxification, often requiring short-term hospitalization (often a 28-day program). Supportive follow-up treatment, individual and family counseling and referral to established groups such as Alcoholics Anonymous, Alanon and Alateen are significant components of such programs. Family members and friends must learn how to avoid unknowingly reinforcing the addiction, which means recognizing and addressing their own co-dependency.

The first and most important step toward overcoming alcoholism is breaking through the defense of denial and accepting self-responsibility. Treatment is possible only when the alcoholic is able to recognize that alcoholism is a disease. Once this breakthrough is made, an individual, comprehensive treatment program can be initiated. Such a program should, ideally, include the following components:

The first and most important step toward overcoming alcoholism is breaking through the defense of denial and accepting self-responsibility.

Detoxification

If the alcoholic is unable to stop the use of alcohol without experiencing physical distress, the body is physiologically dependent, and an in-patient detoxification program under medical supervision is required. Most such programs require a 28-day hospitalization.

Individual Counseling and Therapy

Immediately following detoxification, counseling and therapy are important for developing new insights, self-awareness and self-acceptance. These are the building blocks of self-esteem. Old belief systems must be deprogrammed, and new responsibilities for life must be developed. This process of growing awareness includes:

○ A focus on the history of the alcoholic behavior, including when and why it began in the first place. The alcoholic must confront the key emotional issues that underlie the compulsive drinking before new, healthy patterns of coping behavior can be established.

○ The alcoholic must relearn the basic emotions of compassion and self-love. Ultimately, this process includes reaching out to those the alcoholic abused while under the influence. This is central to building a new foundation of love, respect and trust, as well as revitalizing the alcoholic's long-standing lack of self-esteem.

○ For many alcoholics, one of the keys to treatment is learning to confront the compulsive aspects of their personalities, and learning to redirect those aspects of the personality into more productive areas.

Family Counseling and Therapy

It is vital that members of the alcoholic's family become involved with the recovery process. Previous "co-alcoholic" behaviors must be dealt with, and the dynamics of the family explored.

It is vital that members of the alcoholic's family become involved with the recovery process. Previous "co-alcoholic" behaviors must be dealt with, and the dynamics of the family explored.

12-Step Programs

The intensive treatment phase must be followed up by programs that provide ongoing peer support for the recovering alcoholic. The most well-known, and probably the most effective, are 12-step programs such as Alcoholics Anonymous, Alanon, Alateen and Adult Children of Alcoholics.

Diet and Exercise

A health-oriented program of diet and exercise is essential to recovery. Exercise represents an ideal outlet into which the compulsive behaviors of the alcoholic can be redirected.

Assertion Training

The alcoholic must learn effective methods for building self-confidence and discharging anger and negativity. Assertion training can be valuable in defining goals and determining the alcoholic's capabilities and tolerance levels.

Relaxation Training

Progressive relaxation methods such as self-hypnosis and visual imagery can be useful in helping the alcoholic learn to handle stress and anxiety in more productive ways.

Developing a Spiritual Awareness

Spiritual awareness (not necessarily of a religious nature) is also an important aspect of true recovery. Each of us must seek out some higher meaning and purpose to life. It is through the realization and acceptance of the fact that we are not "alone" that chemically dependent individuals can begin to see themselves as part of a larger structure of existence.

Through the realization and acceptance of the fact that we are not "alone," chemically dependent individuals can begin to see themselves as part of a larger structure of existence.

National Resource Directory

National Mental Health Association .... (800) 969-6642

National Depressive and
Manic-Depressive Association .... (800)-826-3632

National Institute of Mental Health .... (800) 421-4211

Summary — Chapter Eight

The three stages of stress
- Alarm stage
- Resistance stage
- Exhaustion stage

Parameters of stress
- Stress is any demand that causes a person to mentally and physically readjust in an effort to maintain a sense of emotional balance.
- The more stable the personality, the better the ability to cope with constant exposure to external demands.
- Some form of stress is experienced by everyone, every day.
- Our own thoughts can generate stress.
- Lack of appropriate coping mechanisms results in further escalation of stress.

Sources of stress
- The need for recognition
- External social/occupational demands
- Personal and family problems
- Dealing with authority
- Emotional communication

Symptoms of stress
- Weight gain/loss
- Combativeness, irritability, impulsiveness, hostility
- Exaggerated sense of despair and fear
- Excessive use of sick leave; job-related injuries
- Excessive use of mood-altering substances
- Marital/family conflict

≡ Sexual dysfunction
≡ Inappropriate responses
≡ Certain health problems
≡ Complaints about financial problems
≡ Feelings of isolation/alienation
≡ Arrogance or overcompensation
≡ Crying spells
≡ Loss of interest in work, family, hobbies
≡ Accidents
≡ Acute or chronic fatigue
≡ Sleep disorders
≡ Other changes from person's "normal" behavior

Anxiety

≡ Anxiety is associated with motor and muscular tension, autonomic nervous system hyperactivity, gastrointestinal symptoms, apprehension and hyper-vigilance.
≡ Anxiety stimulates the adrenal gland to produce adrenaline, causing the "fight-or-flight" syndrome. Symptoms include increased heart and respiratory rates, sweating, blood vessel constriction and dilated pupils.
≡ Exposure to excess adrenaline can be destructive over time.
≡ Suppression or repression of antisocial impulses can also trigger anxiety.
≡ The constant need to block thoughts and feelings and maintain emotional distance prevents communication and increases anxiety.

Compulsive disorders
≡ May be referred to as "addictions," such as excessive eating, bingeing, workaholism, compulsive shopping, compulsive sexual behavior and excessive use of power or authority.

Depression
≡ Depression may be related to Chronic Fatigue Syndrome, which is characterized by fatigue, depression, difficulty communicating, swollen lymph nodes, joint pain, headache, dizziness, sore throat, low grade fever, chest pain and palpitations and upper respiratory and gastrointestinal symptoms.

≡ General symptoms of depression include dysphoric mood; social withdrawal; anxiety, fear and heightened concern about physical ailments; psychomotor retardation and decreased energy; appetite changes; sleep disturbance; low self-esteem and self-worth; thought and information-processing distortion; and suicidal thoughts.

Alcoholism
≡ One in 10 Americans is an alcoholic.
≡ The "skid row" alcoholic is a stereotype; anyone can become an alcoholic.
≡ An alcoholic costs his employer an additional 25 percent over his salary in losses due to absenteeism, reduced efficiency, on-the-job accidents and medical benefits.

≡ Alcoholism may be caused by a genetic predisposition, certain childhood experiences and an attempt to self-medicate anxiety.

≡ Alcoholism leads to blackouts, feelings of guilt, aggressive behavior and increasing tolerance to and reliance on alcohol.

≡ Emotional symptoms include irritability; hostility; impulsiveness; demanding, cynical behavior; mood swings; and difficulty with objective, moral and ethical judgments.

≡ Physical symptoms include bloating, flushed face, red eyes, decreased sexual desire and performance and slowed reflexes, especially eye and hand coordination.

≡ Long-term neurological symptoms include loss of short- and long-term memory, chronic irritability and difficulty with abstract thinking.

Treatment of Alcoholism

≡ Co-dependents should also be treated.

≡ Individual and group counseling provide mutual support.

≡ Detoxification, often a 28-day program, may be necessary.

≡ The alcoholic must give up denial and accept responsibility for the disease.

≡ Other effective treatments include family counseling, individual therapy, 12-step programs, diet and exercise, assertion and relaxation training and developing a spiritual awareness.

Chapter Nine

Working Through a Life Crisis

In every age, "the good old days" were a myth. No one ever thought they were good at the time. For every age has consisted of crises that seemed intolerable to the people who lived through them.

— *Brooks Atkinson*

In September 1989, Hurricane Hugo ripped through the Caribbean, wreaking havoc upon Puerto Rico and the Virgin Islands, ultimately smashing into the Charleston, South Carolina area. Then, in 1992, hurricanes Andrew and Iniki devastated the coastal areas of North Carolina and Hawaii, respectively. Many lost their lives, but even among uninjured survivors, the disasters disrupted routines as basic as working, eating and sleeping. General fatigue and other stressors tested the mental health and endurance of entire communities to the limits.

Many local residents, some of whom had lost all of their worldly possessions, worked around the clock assisting public safety employees and military personnel as they searched for any signs of life among the debris. As they made tremendous sacrifices to help other families whose loved ones had been killed or injured, weeks passed before many of these workers were able to fully assess their own losses. When the crisis finally passed and they began to realize the tremendous impact of the disasters on their own lives, many became disoriented and traumatized. Dealing with the shock of losing friends, neighbors and family members, as well as the general destruction of familiar sights and surroundings, was a major challenge.

Any life-and-death experience leaves a significant emotional imprint. Before we can really cope effectively, we have to undergo a process of "emotional decompression," or distancing from the demands of the crisis situation.

A crisis does not necessarily lead to burnout. However, it most certainly depletes energy and contributes to emotional exhaustion. If the emotional reaction to the crisis is not resolved effectively, burnout can, and often does, occur. Our response to any crisis or traumatic event is dictated by several factors — how we perceive the event, our previous experience in dealing with crises and how many other problems, concerns or conflicts we have in our lives at that particular time.

Typically, the immediate emotional reaction to crisis involves tension and confusion. Psychologically, the future seems uncertain; worse, we may not really understand the reason for these feelings. Even more threatening is the fact that we just don't know how to stop the reaction!

Each of us reacts to crisis differently. For many of us, the reactions are feelings of loneliness, despair, self-absorption and self-pity. Alternatively, we may feel like no one else can possibly understand how isolated we feel, or how much pain we're experiencing. This may lead us to believe that our own reaction to the crisis is "abnormal." Rather than face potential ridicule for exposing our feelings, sometimes we withdraw, in the process isolating ourselves from others. Ultimately, such a coping style blocks the possibility for honest, healthy feedback and comfort, especially from others who have experienced a crisis and can fully understand our behavior and provide us with much-needed emotional support.

Any life-and-death experience leaves a significant emotional imprint. Before we can really cope effectively, we have to undergo a process of "emotional decompression," or distancing from the demands of the crisis situation.

CASE HISTORY   Sylvia R.

At age 16, Sylvia R. was severely injured in an automobile accident. She was driving when the accident occurred, with her family as passengers. Suddenly, at 65 miles an hour, a tire came off, causing their truck to overturn. Sylvia was thrown to the pavement. She lay comatose and close to death for two weeks. She was paralyzed because of spinal damage, and required brain surgery and skin grafting. Two years of intensive medical care with repeated surgeries brought about minimal recovery. To this day, she experiences a sleep disorder, mentally replaying the trauma and its aftermath in her mind.

"It took five years for us to get our day in court. The jury trial lasted 10 weeks. It was really complicated, with the tire company bringing in its experts about tires, roads, vehicles and mechanics. The tire that blew out was gone, either disintegrated or stolen. According to the company's attorneys, the accident was all my fault. They said my inexperience as a driver caused the tire to separate from the rim on that desert highway.

"Here I was, a teenager, standing up against this powerful tire manufacturer and other companies. I felt really persecuted. I was the one who had had my life torn apart, and all I was doing was driving with my family. I felt like we had every right to expect the tire company that made the bad tire to make up for some of the damage that had already been done.

"The jury deliberated for three days, and I was positive justice would be served — how could they not decide in our favor? But when the jury room buzzer finally rang and the jury filed in, they had found in favor of the tire people. My family and I were devastated. We were left with nothing but five years worth of attorney fees!

"This experience created within me a desire to learn about and become aware of all aspects of life. I feel that there must be a purpose for me surviving the accident. This feeling of purpose has given me the strength to live with the injustice of it all. I'm sure it will help me deal with difficulties more effectively later on in my life as well."

Definition of a Life Crisis

A crisis may be defined as an acute stress situation that is a threat to our sense of self. Typical situations or events that may trigger a crisis reaction include:

- A major disaster involving an entire community, such as a flood, tornado, earthquake or air crash
- Sudden death of a family member, especially a child
- The loss of one's home, e.g., through fire, earthquake, storm
- An acute traumatic injury or illness resulting in a chronic physical disability
- Sudden loss of job or a job-threatening situation, including business takeover, layoffs, malpractice lawsuits, work injury

In the middle of a crisis, we don't generally understand what's happening or what might happen to us. Distorted perceptions are common. Other typical responses include depression, confusion, anxiety, feelings of panic and fear.

A crisis can, and usually does, strike suddenly. We may be a casual bystander, not directly involved with the specific incident (such as witnessing a traumatic auto accident), but still suffer a crisis reaction. When we are in the middle of a crisis, we don't generally understand what is happening or what might happen in the immediate future. Distorted perceptions are common. Other typical responses include depression, confusion, anxiety, foreboding, feelings of panic, fear of impending loss and shock.

In helping a loved one or a peer (or even ourselves) through a crisis, it is important to recognize the following psychological and emotional reactions to a crisis:

- A loss of sense of reality and ability to adequately differentiate between our emotional state and the realities of the external world

- Feelings of helplessness that serve to increase tension even further: "Why can't I relieve this horrible feeling?"
- Refusal to acknowledge emotions such as anxiety or physical symptoms
- Inability to predict or anticipate future events
- No clear understanding of the cause of an event; inability to address the question: "What will happen to me next?"
- Loss of psychological and emotional equilibrium, often followed by renewed efforts to cope

Most of us will experience several crises during our lives, and it is important to be prepared. While reactions to crisis often involve anxiety and depression, the negative effects of these emotions can be relieved by understanding their causes.

While reactions to crisis often involve anxiety and depression, the negative effects of these emotions can be relieved by understanding their causes.

Post-Traumatic Stress and Crisis

Post-Traumatic Stress Disorder (PTSD), characterized by a constant state of emergency and exaggerated biological responses to even minor stressors, was first diagnosed among combat veterans and victims of war. More recently, it has also been identified in children who have witnessed violence, victims of rape and other crimes and public safety personnel who have dealt with or experienced violent incidents.

PTSD results from exposure to an identifiable traumatic event. Examples include battles, air crashes, shootings and floods or other natural disasters. PTSD has been referred to as "battle fatigue," because it can occur in soldiers who have lived through violent combat situations. PTSD is characterized by mentally re-experiencing the crisis situation on an ongoing basis. Most dangerously, the victim of PTSD loses the ability to ever feel safe and out of harm's way.

Symptoms may be appear immediately following the trauma, or may not develop for six months, a year or longer. These symptoms include re-experiencing the traumatic event while awake or asleep (flashbacks), increased irritability, unpredictably aggressive behavior and a physical and emotional distancing from the outside world. Anxiety and depression are generally present, as well as a loss of interest in hobbies or other normal activities. Sleep disturbance and hyper-vigilance are also common.

After living through a major life crisis, we do not perceive the world as orderly and predictable. Instead, we feel trapped in a sense of chaos and imbalance that threatens the very values and assumptions on which we base our lives.

After living through a major life crisis, we do not perceive the world as orderly and predictable. Instead, we feel trapped in a sense of chaos and imbalance that threatens the very values and assumptions on which we base our lives. To cope with these psychological and emotional reactions, sufferers of PTSD sometimes resort to self-medication, using tranquilizers, alcohol or marijuana as a means of repressing memories of the trauma and subsequent emotional reactions.

Post-Traumatic Stress Disorder and burnout are not quite the same, although many of the symptoms are similar. In PTSD, the cause is related to a specific and unusual life event that is acute and identifiable. Burnout, on the other hand, results from the cumulative effects of coping with chronic and often indefinable stressors.

Overcoming a Life Crisis

In most cases, *the passage of time alone* is sufficient to restore healthy psychological and emotional functioning after a crisis. However, it may also be necessary to consult a doctor or therapist to obtain objective insight and emotional support during such periods. This assistance is typically of a short-term (crisis intervention) nature. Often, all that is needed is to learn a new set of coping techniques for dealing with the stress presented by the extraordinary life event creating the crisis.

After a divorce or the breakup of a relationship, for example, we may feel completely alone in the world. Emotional support from others is needed to fill the void and reduce the isolation, loneliness, despair and need for validation. Family and friends are often the first line of support in such situations.

After a divorce or the breakup of a relationship we may feel completely alone in the world. Emotional support from others is needed to fill the void.

Events tend to occur so quickly during a life crisis that we don't have time to develop new behaviors to cope with the related stressors. For this reason, role-playing and other techniques designed to teach new coping skills can be useful in helping the victims of crisis. This kind of help can even be obtained before a crisis occurs, and can be thought of as a psychological inoculation against disaster!

If it is likely that, at some point, a crisis situation will occur in our lives, we can prepare by learning problem-solving methods that allow us to respond appropriately when the time comes. Those with dangerous occupations can be taught methods for assessing their options in the event of an injury or psychological trauma. This involves the use of rational, non-emotional problem-solving to handle the problem and make decisions regarding recovery.

Other stressful events, such as the loss of our home or personal belongings through fire or theft, can be dealt with by assessing the situation from a different perspective. This can take the form of cognitive restructuring, a method of modifying thoughts, perceptions and emotions related to a situation. The result: We learn to re-frame the loss so that grief and despair are not immobilizing. A sense of thankfulness to be alive and hope for rebuilding can foster a more positive attitude about our acute life situation.

Another important aspect of crisis intervention is to counteract the expected psychological and emotional withdrawal by helping the victim reach out and share the sense of grief, loss and despair. A major step in restoring psychological and emotional balance is to link our personal loss to losses suffered by others.

Deriving a sense of meaning and purpose from suffering, as well as understanding the nature of our own grief, can provide the strength needed for survival.

Believe it or not, life crises can have a long-term positive impact. For example, a recent study of high school students who had suffered life crises such as gang violence or the death of friends indicated that 87 percent of those studied later developed a more-positive view of life. The researchers stressed that many people have the ability to transcend pain and adversity, a position previously under-emphasized in other studies. In other words, cognitive changes were brought about by these individuals' own painful experiences, changes that provided a means by which their understanding of life's meaning could grow.

During a crisis, the courage to continue with life even while suffering personal grief is nurtured by providing compassion and help to others. A prime example is the founding of the group Mothers Against Drunk Drivers (MADD). MADD was founded by a Texas woman whose daughter had been fatally injured by a drunk driver; instead of withdrawing into her own loss, despair and self-pity, she discovered that there were hundreds of other families who shared her grief and decided to do something about it. MADD now sponsors support groups for families who have been victims of drunk drivers, as well as funds national cam-

Deriving a sense of meaning and purpose from suffering, as well as understanding the nature of our own grief, can provide the strength needed for survival.

paigns against drinking and driving. Essentially, she utilized a personal act of compassion to focus on the needs of others who had suffered similar losses, thus accelerating her own process of self-healing.

It is interesting to note that the Chinese ideogram for "crisis" and "dangerous opportunity" are the same. A crisis can be seen as testing our attitudes, resources and creativity. Just as maintaining our physical, emotional and mental health helps us to take full advantage of positive opportunities, it will also facilitate our coping with a life crisis. It allows not only for more effective short-term coping — but also aids us in turning adversity into personal growth. 📖

Crisis tests our attitudes, resources and creativity. Maintaining physical, emotional and mental health allows us to take advantage of positive opportunities. It helps us cope with life crises.

CASE HISTORY   Mary B.

Mary B. got married in her early thirties. She came from a close Catholic family, and her husband was openly and warmly accepted. After only a few years of a happy marriage, her husband developed a terminal illness. He was hospitalized for lengthy periods, and Mary would make daily visits, accompanied by various members of her family. On the way to one of these visits, her husband's mother suffered a fatal heart attack in the car. Mary had to handle the arrangements while keeping the news from her husband, who was rapidly deteriorating. He died two weeks later. Less than a month later, Mary's own mother suffered a stroke, was hospitalized for a month and then died.

Faced with tremendous adversity, Mary was able to keep coping and surviving. She attributes her strength to the strong values and spiritual support provided by her family.

"Of course it was all horrible and terrifying. But the strength of my family and our deep religious devotion helped me deal with the stress. I am a very quiet person, but my quietness comes from an inner strength. It's not necessary to always impress other people that you're able to be in control. Only you have to know that you can control your own emotions and deal with difficulties. When you truly believe that there is something greater and more beautiful than anything you might be or hope for, this belief can carry you through tragedies and hard times. My religious beliefs helped me face the death of several of the most important people in my life. Faith helps a person face death. I know that it will also help me face my own death when the time comes, as well."

CASE HISTORY   Bill S.

Bill S., a 55-year old cosmetologist, was faced with a major decision about whether to continue his successful business after the stress it generated created a real and very serious health risk. Bill came to the correct conclusion that he'd been doing something with his life that made him unhappy. His decision to change — to stop being driven by the expectations of others — allowed him to redesign his lifestyle.

"I was never a super achiever, having only a high school education. I became a cosmetologist because I got along with people, and women in particular. After working for someone for years, I went into business with an acquaintance, whom I bought out after six months. Business was good, and I soon had three shops. All it meant was that I'd entered a rat race, 14-hour days, six days a week. I never asked for all that responsibility, but everyone I knew was ambitious and trying to hit the big time. I just went along, and it got more and more stressful.

"Then it all came crashing down. I hadn't been feeling well, but I refused to go in for a check-up. One day I got very ill, and was rushed to the emergency room, where they told me I'd lost half my blood to bleeding ulcers. They gave me transfusions that saved my life.

"I didn't work for a month or so after that, and decided that nothing was worth endangering my health. I'd always done what the world expected of me, but I realized that something had to change. The very next week I just closed my shops.

"When I went to the doctor a month later, there was no trace of the ulcer that had threatened my life. He asked what I'd done, and I told him I'd gotten rid of the problem that caused the ulcer. Now I work for someone else part-time. I don't make nearly the money, but I have my health and I'm happy. If I hadn't made the change, I think I'd be dead today."

SUMMARY — CHAPTER NINE

Crisis defined
≡ A crisis is an acute stress situation that is a threat to the sense of self.
≡ Crises include major disasters involving entire communities, sudden death of a family member, loss of one's home, acute traumatic injury or illness or sudden loss of job or a job-threatening situation.
≡ Victims must undergo "emotional decompression" before healing can take place.

Symptoms of crisis
≡ Tension and confusion, loneliness, despair, self-absorption and self-pity
≡ Loss of sense of reality
≡ Feelings of helplessness
≡ Denial of anxiety or physical symptoms
≡ Inability to predict or anticipate future events
≡ Loss of psychological and emotional equilibrium, often followed by renewed efforts to cope

Post-Traumatic Stress Disorder
≡ PTSD is characterized by a constant state of emergency and exaggerated biological responses to even minor stressors.
≡ It stems from exposure to an identifiable traumatic event.

≡ Victims include combat veterans and victims of war, those who have witnessed violence, victims of rape and other crimes and public safety personnel who have dealt with traumatic accidents.

≡ Onset of symptoms may be delayed.

≡ Symptoms include flashbacks, irritability, unpredictable aggression and physical or emotional distancing.

Overcoming crisis

≡ Passage of time may be sufficient.

≡ Short-term crisis intervention may be necessary.

≡ Role-playing and other coping techniques may be helpful, or cognitive restructuring, that is, assessing the situation from a different perspective.

≡ It is possible to learn effective problem-solving skills *before* a crisis occurs.

≡ The victim should be encouraged to reach out and communicate grief, loss and despair.

≡ Crises can be turned into an opportunity for personal growth.

Chapter Ten

Burnout — A Modern American Epidemic

Just as the hand, held before the eye, can hide the tallest mountain, so the routine of everyday life can keep us from seeing the vast radiance and the secret wonders that fill the world.

— Chassidic proverb, 18th century

Americans tend to define their identities in terms of their professions or occupations. The pressure to succeed — to attain the American Dream — is centered largely in the economic arena, and many people spend their lives chasing acceptability and approval in the business or professional worlds. This implies that events that occur on the job may have a significant impact on other areas of our lives. For example, it is all too common for the pressure generated by problems in today's workplace to spill over to our personal lives, creating difficulties in marriage, family and other non-work relationships.

It has been postulated that those with careers in such fields as medicine, law enforcement or public safety tend to define their self concept largely in terms of their social and occupational role. However, this problem actually exists for most of us. Unfortunately, this over-identification with our work role may reach its apex in burnout.

Although *burnout* is not yet included in standard psychiatric manuals, a primary clinical profile can be identified. Burnout is a state of exhaustion resulting from the interaction of:

º Pre-existing personality factors
º Predisposing factors (such as poor coping skills)
º Psychological needs and expectations
º Life experiences
º Environmental conditions

Emotional Emptiness and Burnout

In our society, Utopian values like self-expression, culture and development of the human spirit are not considered relevant. Instead, money and material goods are the yardstick by which we measure success and, ultimately, self-worth.

We live in a highly acquisitive society, in which personal happiness and satisfaction are seen as directly related to the acquisition of material possessions. This primary value is always there, defining the ideal of achievement and success. Utopian values like self-expression, culture and development of the human spirit are not considered relevant. Instead, money and material goods are the yardstick by which we measure success and, ultimately, self-worth. The "Me Generation" is fixated with materialism and the acquisition of "things," leading ultimately to feelings of emptiness and depersonalization. "Things" can never fill us up or provide us with meaning and purpose in life.

Another flawed aspect of our society's value system is the need for stimulation. We constantly demand distraction — *entertain me now!* We don't like the feeling we get when work or other activities are unstimulating — it's as if there's an emotional void that has to be filled up to validate our existence. Rather than figuring out our own true needs and wants, we seek fulfillment through the approval of others. Even worse, we tend to seek out this validation from other overworking, over-spending, compulsive people.

The bottom line is that these behaviors serve to distract us from our own inner thoughts and feelings. We must ultimately learn what will really bring us happiness.

Identifying Burnout Behavior

We all live with anxiety in our daily lives — Can we meet our monthly expenses? Will our car break down? Will we have enough money to send the kids to a good college? These kinds of worries have been with us for generations, and, for the most part, we've all grown up expecting to face such anxieties. A certain amount of anxiety is normal, and mild to moderate levels of anxiety may even be stimulating and motivating.

A certain amount of anxiety is normal, and mild to moderate levels of anxiety may even be stimulating and motivating. Living in our modern world brings with it a number of anxieties about situations over which we have little or no control.

However, living in our modern world brings with it a number of anxieties about situations *over which we have little or no control.* Might we be shot in an incident of random violence? Will our teenage child get strung out on drugs and try to commit suicide? Will our company merge and our department and job of 20 years suddenly vanish? Will someone we love die of AIDS? Paranoia? Not exactly. One look at the daily paper shows that these anxieties have an all-too-real basis in fact.

We all have to deal with these anxieties, and we all cope in different ways. Some of us, to the tune of at least 10 million prescriptions annually, turn to tranquilizers such as Valium to quiet our jangled nerves. Many self-medicate with their drug of choice, be it alcohol, pot or cocaine. Others become workaholics, working as many hours as they can squeeze out of body and mind.

Personality and the Burnout Process

Our personality determines the degree of likelihood that we will become burned out, as well as the specific form it will take. One recent study found that personality characteristics were even more important than occupation in predicting whether burnout would occur. Four personality characteristics in particular were found to increase the risk of burnout:

Boundary Problems at Work

Those of us who identify too strongly with our occupation derive our self-definition from work. There is no clear self-concept apart from the work-related identity, and this can lead to a loss of the sense of "I"-ness. When problems occur at work, they have a direct, negative impact on our self-concept. In contrast, those of us whose self-concept exists *independently* from what we do for a living are much better able to maintain the crucial psychological distance between work and personal life. In these circumstances, we feel less of a need to obtain validation from the work setting, and are more likely to be introspective, that is, oriented toward self-discovery and personal growth.

Lack of Closure

Individuals who have difficulty "closing" or finishing what they start may feel a great compulsion to finish a project. As a result, they are likely to become anxious when something doesn't get finished on time

Self-investment

If we have less concern for the monetary rewards linked to a job, and instead ask, "What can I give to my job?" regardless of whether it's really worth it financially, we may be prone to burnout. In this case, our primary satisfaction comes from the sense of having sacrificed ourselves to our job.

Self-confrontation

If we fall in this category, we may perceive our work as an opportunity for self-testing, and believe that our work efforts represent the only significant arena in which we can prove ourselves worthy.

Burnout and Loss of Self-identity

When we are burned out, we are likely to be very unclear about our self-identity. We lack balance in our personal, social and occupational lives. We become consumed by the repetition of the same stressful and miserable scenes played out day after day. As our internal pressure mounts, we become increasingly dissatisfied with life, asking, "What's the point of it all?"

When we are burned out, we are likely to be very unclear about our own self-identity. We lack balance in our personal, social and occupational lives.

Despite the daily build-up of anxiety and energy that demands to be discharged, we have to keep up and deal with the pressures of day-to-day life. Meanwhile, the internal pressure continues to build. Eventually, coping mechanisms can no longer hold back the waves of fear and despair. "Meaning" and "purpose" in life become shallow concepts, and we lose all interest in improving our ability to cope. Many burnout victims just *give up entirely.*

The profound feelings of helplessness and hopelessness lead to a form of psychological and emotional paralysis. The whole array of burnout symptoms appear — anxiety, depression, low frustration tolerance and hostility. In the most severe cases of burnout, our will to live is so utterly compromised that death is accepted as a viable option for escaping our sense of total misery.

One common reaction is a strong desire to withdraw or escape. This can result in passive withdrawal — perhaps getting fired from work, being careless and thus becoming an accident victim or even being "accidentally" killed.

CASE HISTORY   Joan M.

Joan M. had been employed for seven years as a medical office administrator when she found that she could no longer handle the stress generated by her employers. If you look at how Joan dealt with the building frustration and anger, you can see that she should have done something sooner — much sooner. She waited until it was too late to salvage her self-esteem and even her job.

"We were in the process of purchasing a home. I had a newborn at home, two other kids, and my husband had just changed careers. All those changes happening at once. At work, as an administrator at a medical group, my physician bosses kept putting pressure on me, constantly expanding my job duties. They kept saying, "Joan, you can handle it." I went along with it for years, but the workload just kept getting heavier. I finally rebelled and told them I absolutely had to have an assistant. They kept putting off hiring the help I needed, and I just kept getting more and more stressed out. This went on for about six months.

"Finally, something happened that just pushed me over the edge. One of the physicians asked me to help out in X-ray when I was in the middle of a million administrative tasks. I refused his request, telling him it simply wasn't part of my job. His reaction: 'You've got to do it. You have no choice. Either that or just go for the door.'

"I'd given them seven years of my life, and was shocked that he could say this so casually. I said: 'How can you say that? It's not my job. I'm the office manager.' I told him I was leaving, and he said, 'Then leave!'

"After I left, I started sobbing and shaking, and was barely able to drive. I pulled over to get a grip on myself. I cried for what seemed like hours.

"I always felt I could handle any amount of pressure, but I was wrong. I thought I could handle three kids, a demanding job, a new house and my husband's transitions. All of a sudden, however, I had to face the fact that I couldn't handle all of those stressful things at once."

The All-encompassing Effects of Burnout

Burnout affects all areas of its victim's life, with substantial implications for the psychological (mind), physical (body) and occupational (job) realms. In addition, burnout significantly impacts family life.

Burnout affects all areas of its victim's life, with substantial implications for the psychological, physical and occupational realms.

Psychological Effects of Burnout

Psychologically, many aspects of depression and anxiety come into play during the acute phase of burnout. These include:

Psychological Exhaustion, Mental Fatigue, Loss of Motivation

The inclination is to just sit around in a dull fog. Doing anything that isn't *absolutely* necessary becomes almost impossible. It's like we're being controlled by events swirling around us, and it's just too much effort to cope.

Low Level of Tolerance for Frustration and Ambiguity

It's too difficult to put up with hassles or uncertainty, and we have literally no patience for dealing with complications. We feel irritable and aloof, and may find our social lives crumbling. We tend to make snap judgments about other people — this is also a function of lack of patience.

Difficulty Trusting Others

We question their motivations — in the extreme, paranoia sets in.

A Profound Sense of Helplessness and Hopelessness

It gets to the point where it's difficult, maybe even impossible, to visualize positive solutions to our problems, even taken one at a time. The future looks bleak and filled with doom. We may even have thoughts related to death and suicide, followed by feelings of sadness, grief and despair.

Insecurity

The future seems unpredictable and threatening. We don't know what's going to happen, but we have a premonition that it will be terrible and that there won't be a thing we can do about it! Some may react to these feelings with outbursts of rage and anger — these emotional displays are really defenses against inner pain and the need to escape those gnawing feelings of turmoil and anguish.

Outbursts of rage and anger are really defenses against inner pain and the need to escape those gnawing feelings of turmoil and anguish.

Difficulty Accepting the Burnout Condition

There's a sense of disbelief: "This can't be happening to me!"

Physical Effects of Burnout

Physically, burnout affects many parts of the body, with the physical symptoms becoming progressively more severe as the burnout process proceeds.

Extreme Tiredness

Just as psychological exhaustion becomes complete, we lose our physical energy and drive, as well; we're constantly lethargic. The complaint, "*I'm tired all the time!*" is common.

Vulnerability to Illness, Injury and Chronic Pain

Among the many conditions known to be associated with burnout are cardiovascular problems, gastrointestinal disorders, headaches, chronic neck and back pain, hearing difficulties and high blood pressure.

Muscular Tension

We "tense up" at the slightest provocation. This tenseness causes its own physical symptoms, especially headaches and nervous mannerisms.

Insomnia

It's difficult or impossible to get a good night's sleep. Despite chronic exhaustion, it's difficult to rest well. When we awaken, we may find ourselves lying in a pool of sweat and feel even more tired than when we went to sleep.

Occupational Effects of Burnout

Occupationally, burnout often brings with it a whole series of complications:

Occupationally, burnout often brings with it a whole series of complications, including absenteeism, a sense of isolation and poor work performance.

Absenteeism

Psychological and physical symptoms make it harder to get up every day to go to our jobs, and the result is likely to be missed work, depleted sick days, requests for a leave of absence and mental stress disability claims.

A Sense of Isolation

It's extremely difficult to maintain morale, and we begin to feel isolated and alone at work. At the same time, it's discomforting to share these feelings with family and fellow workers.

Poor Performance, Impaired Productivity

Our work output is likely to suffer, and others usually correctly perceive that our performance has fallen off. As a result, there may be a reprimand or disciplinary action, eventually leading to being dismissed.

A Tendency to Over-identify with the Job

We take work-related demands much too personally. Every task becomes a life-and-death matter.

Family Effects of Burnout

In the family, burnout has a number of important negative consequences:

Isolation

Being constantly exhausted and depressed leads to a growing emotional distance from spouse and children.

Strain on Other Family Members

The inability to deal with the hassles of daily life in general puts a great deal of pressure on others in the household, especially the spouse. This leads to an imbalance in the family system and the growth of resentment.

Our inability to deal with the hassles of daily life in general puts a great deal of pressure on others in the household, especially our spouse. This leads to an imbalance in the family system and the growth of resentment about the perceived unfairness of the situation.

Social Distancing

Lethargy makes it a burden to participate in family and social events, further contributing to the sense of isolation. At the same time, we're most likely to avoid events that have the potential to pull the family back together — we just don't have the energy!

Hostility

We may resort to verbal or physical abuse of other family members as a result of impatience and low frustration tolerance.

Diminished Sex Life

Our sexuality suffers due to a lack of interest and energy; when sex does occur, it's likely to be selfishly motivated.

"Scapegoating"

In seeking someone to blame for our burnout symptoms, other family members may be targeted as scapegoats. We blame them for our problems, and they become the victims of *our* tension, frustration and conflict. Eventually, families can be broken apart by the tensions generated by a loved one's burnout.

Other family members may be targeted as scapegoats. Families can be broken apart by the tensions generated by a loved one's burnout.

Summary — Chapter Ten

Setting the stage for burnout
- ≡ Emotional emptiness
- ≡ Over-identification with social and occupational roles
- ≡ Exhaustion
- ≡ Preexisting personality factors such as poor coping skills and psychological needs and expectations
- ≡ Life experiences and environmental circumstances
- ≡ Anxiety about events that cannot be controlled

Personality and the burnout process
- ≡ Boundary problems at work
- ≡ Lack of closure
- ≡ Low degree of self-investment
- ≡ Poor self-confrontation

Psychological effects of burnout
- ≡ Mental exhaustion, loss of motivation
- ≡ Low tolerance for frustration or ambiguity
- ≡ Making snap judgments
- ≡ Decreased trust in others, even paranoia
- ≡ Helplessness, hopelessness
- ≡ Disbelief — "This can't be happening to me!"
- ≡ Depression and anxiety

Physical effects of burnout
- Lack of energy and drive
- Susceptibility to illness, injury and chronic pain
- Muscular tension

Occupational effects of burnout
- Difficulty getting up to go to work, absenteeism
- Poor morale, sense of isolation from co-workers
- Decreased productivity
- Disciplinary reprimand
- Eventual dismissal

Family effects of burnout
- Emotional distancing from spouse and children
- Increased responsibility shifted to other family members, leading to resentment
- Social isolation
- Possible verbal and/or physical abuse
- Diminished sexual drive
- Possible dissolution of the family through separation and divorce

Chapter Eleven

Solutions for Dealing with Burnout

There was that law of life so cruel and so just, which demanded one must grow or else pay dearly for remaining the same.

— *Norman Mailer*

All the available statistics indicate that burnout represents a major threat to the physical and psychological well-being of millions of Americans today. Burnout has reached epidemic proportions, and something has to be done!

Most of us learned early in childhood that we had to battle and always try to come out on top — to get the upper hand in life. Yet, none of us can avoid life's heartbreaks and disappointments.

Dr. Victor Frankl, the world-renowned psychiatrist and founder of Logotherapy, wrote quite movingly about his experiences in Nazi concentration camps, and the positive lessons that he drew from those terrible events. Few of us can even imagine the horrors he experienced, yet Dr. Frankl kept looking for meaning in what was happening to him and millions of other people during this most oppressive and dehumanizing period. After being stripped of all his worldly possessions and isolated from his family, the only power he felt was his control over his own thoughts and attitudes — and his will to survive. One of his most important observations was that those who maintained a will to live, clinging to the belief that their lives still had meaning, significantly increased their chances of survival.

We can't always choose what will happen to us, but we can always choose how we will interpret and respond to those events. We can choose to see ourselves as helpless victims, pointing the finger of blame toward others as we sit on our "pity pot." This serves no good purpose. Being preoccupied with our role as "victim" blinds us to the opportunities that exist in every moment of our life. Nothing can ever happen to us that we can't handle if we prepare ourselves psychologically and emotionally.

Success in dealing with a life crisis requires keeping the present moment sacred, giving up the melodrama and horror story approach, and resisting the temptation to blow events out of proportion. When we are fully alive in the present, we can always deal with the future.

Success in dealing with a life crisis requires keeping the present moment sacred, giving up the melodrama and horror story approach, and resisting the temptation to blow events out of proportion. (Not *everything* is a catastrophe!) When we are fully alive in the present, we can always deal with the future.

As we age, our body tissue breaks down more rapidly under sustained tension. Each stressful event, especially frustrating and unsuccessful struggles, leaves an irreversible chemical "scar." Over time, these bodily insults accumulate and cause our tissue to deteriorate more rapidly. Just as machines without proper maintenance show excessive wear and tear after prolonged use, our physical system will break down under chronic and prolonged stimulation.

To continue the analogy, a heating or cooling system with a broken thermostat can be disastrous. The "feedback" from the thermostat is continuously incorrect, leading to overheating or over-cooling of the system and possibly to a fire or explosion. At the least, the system will wear out much too soon.

The human equivalent is the person whose internal emotional "thermostat" is malfunctioning and providing incorrect feedback. The body responds to those signals, assuming they are correct. It expends far more energy than the situation actually warrants! The cumulative effect of those erroneous signals is likely to be dysphoria — emotional states of anxiety, depression and restlessness. At the extreme level, the body and the "spirit" begin to break down. Stress takes its toll!

Overcoming burnout requires a complete reevaluation of our priorities — occupational/professional, family relationships, basic values and attitudes and long-term goals in life. We must accept the need for imposing balance and moderation and a healthy lifestyle. This means that we must listen to — and heed — our own physical and psychological thermostats. Sometimes just hunkering down and simplifying our lives is all it takes to restore a healthy balance.

Overcoming burnout requires a complete reevaluation of our priorities — occupational/professional, family relationships, basic values and attitudes and long-term goals in life.

The Need for a Fresh Perspective

Each of us has developed our own unique style of coping with the psychological and physical demands placed upon us. Even though those coping methods may have been quite effective for much of our lives, we may find that new problems require new techniques or solutions. We must be flexible and willing to "learn new tricks" if we want to keep functioning at our optimal level and deal effectively with a stressful lifestyle.

We often assume that optimal performance involves the generation of "creative tension," and that anything less should not be accepted. While this may be true for some of us, it can be equally destructive for others. We all have different tolerances for stress and anxiety, and the level of tension that one person can handle may be mentally and physically destructive for someone else.

Quite often, emotional emptiness lies at the core of anxiety or panic attacks. Thoughts that are hidden from the rest of the world and, most fundamentally, from ourselves create the most pain for us. To deal with this emptiness, we must create our own healthy environment in which there is unconditional self-acceptance that allows us to open up and face the truth about who we are and what our pain is all about. We must quit trying to ignore that inner emptiness through distraction, overwork or overindulgence.

Social support is an important aspect of dealing with anxiety. Allowing ourselves to talk about our problems reduces the inner pressure that builds up as a result of constant attempts to cope with stressors and anxiety.

Social support is an important aspect of dealing with anxiety. It is essential to be able to rely on support from family members, friends and business associates when we are in a state of extreme anxiety. Allowing ourselves to talk about our problems — the sources of the anxiety — reduces the inner pressure that builds up as a result of constant attempts to cope with stressors and anxiety. These interactions with others lessen the feelings of isolation and alienation that almost always come with anxiety reactions.

Many of us are reluctant to admit to our stress-related problems or even to recognize that our formerly effective coping methods are no longer effective in dealing with stress overload. However, it is essential that we recognize our own weaknesses and implement systematic strategies for improving our ability to deal with the stressors in our life. It is also important to recognize the other side of the coin — burnout can have subtle *positive* effects, and ultimately be growth-producing. By coping with and overcoming the stressors in our lives, we can develop a new and healthier approach to our existence. Ultimately, we must treat stressful events as challenges, and find ways to transform them into opportunities for personal growth and development.

The Multi-faceted Treatment of Stress and Burnout

Everyone affected by burnout experiences it in a slightly different fashion, and this implies that any treatment plan and intervention should be tailored on an individual basis. Ideally, burnout should be dealt with from a *preventative* rather than a *curative* perspective. And a truly preventative approach involves making fundamental changes in our attitudes and motivations.

While attempting to find someone or something to blame for the burnout condition is a counter-productive exercise, the fact is that burnout victims do not reach a state of total exhaustion totally on their own. Instead, the cumulative effects of occupational, social and family pressures create a catalyst for burnout to occur. The tendency on the part of the burnout victim to deny that any problem even exists only makes matters worse. We must learn to quit suppressing our feelings and communicate openly about our real needs, wants and fears.

There are many different ways in which we can become educated about the negative effects of burnout and how to recognize the early warning signs. Educational programs in the workplace can play a key role in making workers aware of the potential for burnout and of ways they can more effectively handle stress.

Educational programs in the workplace can play a key role in making workers aware of the potential for burnout and of ways they can more effectively handle stress.

Dealing with the wide-ranging and multi-dimensional effects of burnout is no simple matter. Effective intervention requires a well-thought-out strategy that addresses the diverse symptoms — psychological, emotional, occupational and physical.

Individual psychotherapy and family counseling are central to the treatment of burnout. The sense of personal isolation must be overcome in order to allow others to enter the burnout victim's emotional life. Many businesses are beginning to implement programs that incorporate individual and family counseling components.

Vocational rehabilitation is also an important component of a comprehensive treatment program. In many cases of occupational burnout, the effects are so severe that the individual may be forced into early retirement. When this occurs, psychological problems related to the loss of a lifelong occupation must be confronted. Mental, emotional and physical well-being must be restored, along with personal identity and self-worth.

As we attempt to cope with cumulative stress, our energy level frequently borders on exhaustion. *Tremendous amounts of energy are required just to maintain a semblance of emotional balance.*

As we attempt to cope with cumulative stress, our energy level frequently borders on *exhaustion*. Tremendous amounts of energy are required just to maintain a semblance of emotional balance. Performance in both the personal and occupational arenas is seriously compromised. Ultimately, these pressures can build up into the classic burnout syndrome — anxiety, depression, suicidal gestures, despair on a consistent basis or chemical or behavioral addiction seriously impairing our judgment and behavior.

Once burnout has reached this stage, its victims may fear that the only solution is to make major changes in occupational or social responsibilities. This type of major life decision will depend on the specific circumstances. However, a period of rest and distancing from the demands of daily life is, in most cases, absolutely necessary for the burnout victim to regain a sense of emotional, physical and psychological balance.

A Comprehensive Program for Dealing with Stress and Burnout

The following interventions are components of a comprehensive program for dealing with cumulative stress and burnout:

Self-Disclosure, Communication and Catharsis

One symptom of a true anxiety reaction is the blockage of the ability to engage in healthy problem-solving. To overcome our anxiety, we must find a way to release pent-up emotions — then we will be free to explore innovative solutions.

During these stressful periods, we need a trusted friend and a willingness to disclose our innermost feelings. We have to learn to articulate our innermost thoughts about our needs, frustrations and values. Doing so provides a safety valve for our intellectual and emotional systems to decompress.

A Time-out to Gain a Perspective on Life

Being on the front lines of the stress battle for too long inevitably wears us down. The unrelenting adrenal pressure and psychic pain becomes just too much to bear.

Cognitive Restructuring

We can learn to *reframe* situations in our minds so that they are less likely to induce a state of anxiety or depression. This can be highly useful, for example, in coping with anticipatory anxiety about future events. The goal of cognitive restructuring is to reduce or eliminate our negative, automatic thoughts that trigger emotional reactions, replacing them with more positive modes of thinking and problem solving. By consciously imposing a period of time between stimulus and response — a period during which the stressor and its potential consequences can be rationally evaluated — negative thoughts and anxiety can be controlled. Anticipating a future event is perfectly normal, and it's true that problems might develop when the event finally occurs. However, rational thought processes are the first line of defense against this type of anxiety or depression.

The goal of cognitive restructuring is to reduce or eliminate our negative, automatic thoughts that trigger emotional reactions, replacing them with more positive modes of thinking and problem solving.

Tension Reduction Methods

Tension reduction methods are useful for lowering our state of emotional arousal and helping us to restore a sense of psychological, emotional and social balance. Ultimately, the objective is to facilitate improved coping skills and instill a sense of well-being. These strategies, which represent a more aggressive approach to fighting the negative effects of anxiety and the stressors in our life, will be discussed later in this chapter.

Exercise and Nutrition

Regular exercise and proper nutrition are key components of most approaches to reducing tension and anxiety. While it takes a concentrated effort to reprogram our dietary habits, the benefits will be felt almost immediately. Lowering, and even eliminating, the dietary intake of processed sugar has been shown to reduce the effects of anxiety and depression in both adults and children.

A rigorous and well-designed physical workout program can lead to a heightened sense of well-being and internal calm.

A rigorous and well-designed physical workout program can lead to a heightened sense of well-being and internal calm. These positive feelings can be attributed to the release of endorphins (the body's neurochemical equivalent of morphine) in the brain. Exercise also has a profound effect in treating compulsive disorders, particularly binge eating and depression. Physical activity offers a substitute behavior with far more beneficial results.

When weight loss is an associated goal of a stress reduction program, neither diet nor exercise alone is sufficient to bring about healthy weight loss. Both diet and exercise regimens must be faithfully followed if they are to be effective. This can be related to the body's "set-point" or maintenance level. Individuals trying to lose weight through dietary restriction alone often complain that, at a certain stage, their weight loss reaches a plateau beyond which they cannot progress. This is because the person's metabolism slows down to a certain level to compensate for the reduction in caloric intake (set-point). The most effective means of "tricking" the body's set-point is through a program of regular exercise to speed up the body's metabolism while also giving the heart a healthy workout.

The most effective means of "tricking" the body's set-point is through a program of regular exercise to speed up the body's metabolism while also giving the heart a healthy workout.

Self-directed Approaches for Resolving Stress and Burnout

Here are some specific things you can do:

Take a Spontaneous Vacation
Getting away for a weekend, or leaving the familiarity of the everyday environment, can break the cycle of conditioned responses to the same old pressures and pain.

Help Meet the Emotional Needs of Others
Unselfish actions allow us to shift our focus of attention from our own internal stress, and perhaps gain a new perspective on the seriousness of our own situation as compared to someone else's

Focus on Fine-tuning Awareness
Lessons from the past can be drawn upon to develop sensitivity to changes in our internal state and the conditions that trigger them.

Be Objective About Specific External Life Stressors
Make an honest critique of the way we have handled stressful situations or events in the past.

CASE HISTORY   William W.

You can *teach an old dog new tricks*

William W., 49, was president of one of the nation's largest advertising agencies for over 20 years. His schedule required constant pressure and globe hopping. Four years ago, a life-threatening illness linked to stress forced him to change his lifestyle dramatically.

"You always think it can't happen to you. But if you're under stress long enough, you pay the price. I put job first, and lost the balance between job and private life. The big danger is on the physical side, as I learned. If you don't take care of your body, your whole system breaks down. People warned me, but I had to learn the hard way. I lost control, and just kept running as fast as I could. I was tired and exhausted. I didn't stop to think whether it was all necessary.

"There was no particular trigger to my condition. I was in pain for several months, so I took painkillers. The pain got worse and worse, but I wouldn't talk to doctors about the problem. I had always gone to the doctor only in an emergency, just like driving your car till it breaks before taking it to the shop. Finally, I had to be hospitalized for four days.

"As I recovered, I began to exercise. One morning I was exercising, when I saw some joggers. I had always laughed at joggers before, thinking it a waste of time. But now I was intrigued, and found myself wanting to join them. Before I knew it, I was running down the street. I haven't stopped jogging since. Then I joined a health club (also unheard of in my old life) and now I work out religiously three times a week.

"The changes happened on their own after I started to pay attention to my body and made physical fitness a priority. We forget that we create our own commitments. We get so we can't even sit back for a half hour or go for a walk. I've even learned to relax on weekends, and that music has a very therapeutic effect. Before, I just listened to music as background for work. I'd be reading, talking on the phone, watching TV and listening to music all at once. Now I know how to relax, meditate and just enjoy the music."

Imagine That Someone Else Is Experiencing Our Problem

If a family member or close friend came to us for help, how would we tell them to deal with their situation? Write down solutions to the "friend's" problem.

Look at the Problem from All Perspectives

Imagine that your problem is a three-dimensional object in space. How does our behavior affect our own well-being? How does it affect others?

Become Aware of Problems and Stressors

Our efforts to deal with stress will be blocked if we are reluctant to face the problem or deny that anything is wrong. Even those suffering from acute anxiety and tension, decreased motivation, depression and/or fatigue commonly deny that they have a problem. Breaking through that denial and acknowledging that our lives are out of balance is the first and crucially important step toward making the changes needed to reduce stress.

Even those suffering from acute anxiety and tension, decreased motivation, depression and/or fatigue commonly deny that they have a problem.

First of all, we must adjust our "internal thermostats" to track stress accurately and increase our self-awareness. Accurately monitoring the level of stress in our lives is essential, but it can be quite difficult when the "thermostat" has been damaged.

It can be helpful to seek feedback from a trusted person, preferably our significant other. It's important to communicate feelings — negative as well as positive — to others with whom we are emotionally close. Discuss the realization that something is amiss. We can ask loved ones, family members, friends or peers how they see our behavior. Request an honest answer — this is an important step in opening up our "closed system." This opening up of communication helps crystallize our self-perception and allows us to begin to view ourselves a bit more objectively.

Next, we must objectively look at our attitude toward the stressor, and evaluate the payoffs for maintaining that attitude. More often than we want to admit, we hold attitudes or approaches to life that place us in the role of "victim of circumstance." These attitudes are often carryovers from early childhood experiences, when we developed our own coping methods based on those of important role models. For many of us, the role models we emulated may not have been paragons of mental health themselves, and perhaps we emulated their behavior as pitiful victims of circumstance, constantly wailing, "Poor me!" However, maintaining the role of victim only serves to relieve us of taking responsibility for our own life situations. By honestly and objectively evaluating the negative payoffs for continuing to think in this way, we can begin to understand the sources of our despair. The ultimate result is to begin to exercise control over our own lives to a degree we would never have thought possible before.

> *We must objectively look at our attitude toward the stressor, and evaluate the payoffs for maintaining that attitude. By objectively evaluating the negative payoffs, we can begin to understand the sources of our despair.*

Attitude Adjustment — Resetting the "Internal Thermostat"

An important step toward effectively dealing with our stressors is to lower self-expectations so that they are in line with reality. This doesn't mean giving up our dreams or compromising our integrity. Many of us have an internal belief that lowering our expectations represents something negative — defeat! This is especially true for those with a strong need to acquire material goods and achieve society's standards of "success." Giving up does not equal giving in. However, it's just not healthy to continually push ourselves beyond normal and healthy limits. When this pushing goes on for long periods of time, our bodies usually tell us what our minds don't want to know!

In reality, lowering expectations can be quite beneficial, especially in terms of lowered levels of frustration. There is a direct correlation between expectation — what we want out of life — and the degree of stress we experience. Lower, and more-realistic, expectations can serve to reduce feelings of helplessness and depression.

We must ask ourselves — will occupational success and material acquisitions really fulfill our lives? Are they worth losing our mental and physical health over?

Consider these questions:

o Who am I — really?
o What do I *really* want?
o How much am I prepared to give to attain it?
o How much is enough — or too much?

In addition, the "personal myths" we cherish and hold dear are often an impediment to self-awareness. These beliefs and attitudes are the core of our psychological makeup, influencing the way we view the world and ourselves. One of our most fundamental psychological processes involves the belief system and myths we create about who we are. We have to become aware of these myths, and develop a willingness to alter them if they don't contribute to our positive well-being. Learn to recognize personal myths for the psychological baggage they are and question the basis of these belief systems. Beliefs and fears that are irrational or inconsistent with our actual personality force us to "live a lie," hindering our personal growth and progress in life.

Our self-concept was formed early in life by our parents and other central figures or role models, and earliest social

The "personal myths" we cherish and hold dear are often an impediment to self-awareness. Beliefs and fears that are irrational or inconsistent with our actual personality force us to "live a lie."

interactions shaped our belief systems. The way in which other children related to us and we related to them had a significant impact on the social skills we possess today. Our sense of competence and self-worth also spring from these early life experiences. Much of our stress originates from maintaining and defending an early acquired family belief system that may be obsolete in our adulthood. Psychological defenses developed during childhood often operate independently of our conscious awareness and have little to do with protecting us from the problems and conflicts we experience in adult life. Identifying the negative by-products of these defenses is an essential step toward self-mastery.

To get started:

o Make a written list of personal fears.
o Assess how realistic they are in light of our actual identity and accomplishments.
o Ask: "Are these real fears, based on real-life experiences, or are they carryovers from childhood?"
o Consider whether the fears are directly adapted from a role-model.
o Discuss this list with someone who cares about us; assess its validity.

Many burnout sufferers tend to limit their interactions with others according to a strict set of internal rules and regulations. There may be a tendency to see the world as bipolar, with distinct black-white/good-bad evaluations.

Many burnout sufferers tend to limit their interactions with others according to a strict set of internal rules and regulations. There may be a tendency to see the world as bipolar, with distinct black-white/good-bad evaluations. This perspective is unrealistic, and optimal mental health requires that we recognize the gradations along the continuum from positive to negative. *There are gray areas in life,* and failing to recognize and integrate them leads to distorted perceptions and a very limited perception of reality.

Finally, in addition to "cleaning house" on our negative mental attitudes, it is essential to develop a positive attitude toward our physical health. The mind-body link cannot be ignored. Maintaining a healthy body by combining regular exercise with a proper diet is essential for reducing stress. Exercise reduces the internal pressure that accompanies stress. While high levels of stress may cause a lack of energy or motivation to follow an exercise regimen, getting started is the key. Once a systematic program has begun, stress immediately begins to be alleviated.

A proper physical health program requires that tobacco, alcohol and fatty, cholesterol-rich foods be avoided. A compelling reason for burnout sufferers to discontinue fatty foods is that, because of the excess of adrenaline in the blood system during periods of stress, fatty acids don't get metabolized properly, and cholesterol is reduced to pellet-like molecules that attach to and block coronary arteries and veins. Thus, stress coupled with cholesterol-rich foods further increases the risk of coronary heart disease.

Relaxation Techniques

Certain relaxation techniques are quite effective in counteracting the physical effects of anxiety. These methods work by being "antagonistic" to the stimulation of the adrenal response, based on the principle that it is impossible to be both anxious and relaxed at the same time (that is, anxiety and relaxation are antagonistic to one another). By learning to employ appropriate relaxation methods, we basically substitute a relaxation response to a certain stimuli for an anxiety response. Here are some of the most commonly employed and useful relaxation methods:

Relaxation techniques work by being "antagonistic" to the stimulation of the adrenal response, based on the principle that it is impossible to be both anxious and relaxed at the same time.

Progressive Relaxation

In progressive relaxation, each part of the body is progressively and systematically tightened and relaxed, usually from the feet upward. This is done while lying down and breathing from the diaphragm. The breathing and muscle relaxation should be in a matched rhythm, with the goal of achieving reduced tension and a state of deep body relaxation. If properly done, it is possible to remain fully alert and focused on the problem-solving task at hand while practicing progressive relaxation.

Breathing Exercises

The rapid, shallow breathing that frequently occurs during acute anxiety attacks impedes the healthy exchange of oxygen and carbon dioxide, and can result in hyperventilation.

Breathing exercises are effective in compensating for the shallow breathing that often accompanies anxiety. The rapid, shallow breathing that frequently occurs during acute anxiety attacks impedes the healthy exchange of oxygen and carbon dioxide, and can result in hyperventilation.

The effective use of breathing exercises, which are often employed by singers, actors and athletes, requires training in using the diaphragm to breathe at an evenly timed rate. The exercises should be practiced daily, so that when anxiety or stress-provoking stimuli are encountered, they can be immediately employed to restore a healthy respiratory balance. Maximum benefits are gained by lying in a supine position and relaxing the chest muscles and abdominal areas while breathing in and out. This technique is especially helpful during panic attacks and acute anxiety reactions.

Meditation

Meditation, which has been found to be quite effective in alleviating the effects of anxiety, can take many forms; the most appropriate method depends on individual needs. However, in general, meditation is a technique for *centering* total mental effort on one quiet and peaceful aspect of consciousness. During the meditation process, all energies are focused on a level of thought free from value judgments or awareness of self. Meditation, once mastered, can be accomplished in almost any setting, including the workplace.

During the meditation process, all energies are focused on a level of thought free from value judgments or awareness of self.

Systematic Desensitization

Systematic desensitization is useful in dealing with specific fears or anxieties. Start by developing a hierarchy of fear-producing situations. Evaluate all the things that might produce fear, and then rank them according to how potentially frightening they are. At the bottom of this hierarchy are situations with a low potential for producing anxiety, while higher up are situations that would typically cause immobilizing fear or panic. After developing the hierarchy, use visual imagery to substitute a relaxation response for the anxiety reaction these situations usually generate.

Hypnosis

When facilitated by an experienced practitioner, hypnosis, often referred to as "auto-suggestion" or "hyper-suggestibility," can be effective in modifying unhealthy thought and behavior patterns. A hypnotic state is a deep state of relaxation and heightened suggestibility. In contrast to being asleep, the hypnotized person remains aware of surroundings and in control of reactions. Hypnosis can reduce anxiety by neutralizing the stimuli that trigger the anxiety response in the first place.

Hypnosis is valuable for uncovering and modifying unhealthy psychological defenses and producing more-open, less-fearful patterns of thought and behavior. Contrary to popular belief, hypnotized individuals will not say or do things that are at odds with their own values. Hypnotic tech-

Hypnosis can be effective in modifying unhealthy thoughts and behaviors. Hypnotic techniques may be appropriate when basic relaxation methods do not control anxiety.

niques may be appropriate when basic relaxation methods are not effective in controlling anxiety. Hypnosis can also be useful in uncovering early life experiences that contributed to current maladaptive coping behaviors. Therapists who use hypnosis must carefully watch for bodily stress signals, and teach the client how to relax and modify external or internal signals that previously led to the anxiety response.

Community Resources

When the burnout sufferer needs more help than family, friends and self-efforts can accomplish, community-based resources can be accessed to aid in recovery. These resources may be sponsored by the workplace, church or synagogue or social agencies.

If the burnout victim's employer already has a program to treat employees and families experiencing stress, half the battle is won. Some companies have established employee assistance programs (EAPs), many of which have stress units at departmental levels. Other employers use the services of trained and experienced professionals within the community.

Of course, all of these efforts are made more difficult if the burnout victim fails to acknowledge that a problem exists. Usually, the person who needs help has to make the initial contact with these resources. It has been shown that those who realize they are not coping effectively and seek out counseling or psychotherapy often show a more favorable treatment outcome than those who are steered into therapy without recognizing how badly they need help. Generally, experience has shown that counseling sessions are most effective when conducted on a once-per-week basis, especially if the counselee is experiencing an acute crisis or intense emotional reaction.

The initial goal of the counselor is to see the world through the eyes of the individual under stress. Success in establishing this rapport is essential if the counseling is to be effective.

Psychological counseling can incorporate a number of treatment methods that have been shown to be successful in the treatment of stress and burnout. These include:

Supportive Therapy

The primary objectives of this therapy are to provide reassurance and emotional support, as well as to help the stressed-out individual understand the nature of the problem. This includes developing an awareness of what the person can expect to feel or experience as a result of the emotional crisis or burnout condition. It is also important to review the emotional stages likely to be encountered before a resolution is reached.

Uncovering Maladaptive Defense Mechanisms

The therapist helps to identify the unconscious ways in which the burnout victim has been practicing denial. We must recognize the psychological defenses that we use to protect our egos from perceived threats, and learn to develop more effective ways of coping.

We must recognize the psychological defenses that we use to protect our egos from perceived threats, and learn to develop more effective ways of coping.

Assertion Training

Assertion training can facilitate personal growth and behavior change by teaching ways to express personal beliefs, feelings and thoughts without experiencing feelings of guilt, self-condemnation or fear of rejection. Being assertive — learning to express feelings openly and honestly — leads to a sense of personal integrity and increased self-worth. In a sense, it is a purging of pent-up emotions and fear of confrontation.

Crisis Intervention

In extreme stress reactions, crisis intervention can neutralize an intense emotional and/or behavioral reaction to a specific stressor. Crisis intervention may involve removing the stressed individual from his surroundings, and, in some cases, short-term hospitalization may be necessary. This is usually required in cases where the symptoms are severe (e.g. cardiac distress, angina, gastrointestinal conditions, major depression or other acutely disabling disorders).

Marital and Family Counseling

Marital and family therapy allows all family members to openly discuss aspects of the family that may contribute to tension within the household, and how those aspects of the family system can be altered. The therapist acts as a mediator, and works with each family member individually and with the family as a group.

Sick-Leave, Vacation or Holiday Time or Leave of Absence

Distance from the stressor provides time for a new perspective. Threatening situations may be reframed as having minimal consequences.

A temporary change of environment may help the burned-out employee develop a new perspective and coping skills. Creating a distance from the stressor (psychonoxious environment) provides time for a more rational perspective to be developed. Situations perceived as threatening may be reframed as having minimal consequences.

Medical Intervention

When symptoms of anxiety and depression are extremely high, our attention and concentration spans are short, and this can limit the beneficial aspects of counseling and psychotherapy. When psychological efforts prove ineffective in resolving a cumulative stress reaction, a medical examination can provide a comprehensive mental and physical evaluation to rule out contributing physical or other disorders.

When psychological efforts prove ineffective in resolving a cumulative stress reaction, a medical examination can provide a comprehensive mental and physical evaluation to rule out contributing physical or other disorders.

In some cases, psychological or behavioral approaches alone may not reduce the clinical symptoms of stress. In some advanced or aggravated stress reactions, it may be necessary to implement medical treatment. Tranquilizers, antidepressant medications or mood elevators may be used to reduce the effects of extreme anxiety and/or depression. This is the treatment of choice should the individual harbor thoughts of suicide, homicide or other antisocial acts.

Summary — Chapter Eleven

Solutions for burnout
- ≡ Develop a fresh perspective.
- ≡ Determine individual tolerance for "creative tension."
- ≡ Create a healthy environment with unconditional self-acceptance and openness to life's truths.
- ≡ Benefit from a social support system.
- ≡ Recognize personal weaknesses.
- ≡ Implement systematic coping strategies
- ≡ Treat stressful events as a challenge and opportunity for growth.

Professional treatment
- ≡ Intervention should be tailored on an individual basis.
- ≡ The ideal approach should be preventative rather than curative.
- ≡ Educational programs in the workplace are beneficial.
- ≡ Treat psychological, emotional, occupational and physical symptoms.
- ≡ Supportive counseling and individual therapy are necessary.
- ≡ Vocational rehabilitation is an important component.
- ≡ A period of distancing from the demands of daily life may be called for.

Steps of a comprehensive program
- ≡ Self-disclosure, communication and catharsis
- ≡ Take a time-out to gain a perspective
- ≡ Cognitive restructuring
- ≡ Tension reduction methods
- ≡ Exercise and nutrition

Attitude restructuring

- Become aware of the problem or stressor.
- Track stress accurately and increase self-awareness.
- Communicate openly with significant others.
- Evaluate payoffs for maintaining present relationship with stressor.
- Align self-expectations with reality.
- Examine personal myths.
- Allow for gray areas in thinking.
- Develop a positive attitude about physical health.
- Uncover maladaptive defense mechanisms

Relaxation techniques

- Progressive relaxation
- Breathing exercises
- Meditation
- Systematic desensitization
- Hypnosis

Community/Workplace resources

- Employee assistance programs (EAPs)
- Supportive therapy
- Assertion training
- Crisis intervention
- Marital and family counseling
- Sick leave, vacation/holiday time, leave of absence
- Medical intervention

Postscript

I have no teaching. I only point to something. I point to reality. I point to something in reality that had not, or had too little, been seen. I take him who listens to me by the hand and lead him to the window. I open the window and point to what is outside.

— *Martin Buber*

Putting Burnout on the Back Burner

The degree to which we are able to effectively handle the demands and frantic pace of today's society determines how likely we are to encounter burnout. Just because we work under stressful conditions, undergo a major life crisis or are facing traumatic family issues doesn't necessarily mean that we'll end up burned out. The way in which we perceive and react to our own stressors determines that. The main point is that *there are healthy alternatives* and ways of dealing with stress, anxiety and depression. However, it is ultimately up to each one of us to make the decision to give up our denial or unrealistic expectations. Otherwise, no treatment method can be effective in helping us restore a healthy balance to our lives.

Even at the most basic, cellular level, harmony and cooperation are the essence of life. When there is an unease or lack of serenity and peace within a cell, a condition of disease (dis-ease) or disharmony occurs that will eventually kill that cell, and then the surrounding tissue. The chain of events this triggers will eventually destroy the whole human body. The answer to the diseases affecting our bodies and our society is

Negative, automatic thinking must be replaced by a healthy value system that is exclusively our own.

internal and external harmony. We must develop a positive, proactive approach to our inner and outer lives. Negative, automatic thinking must be replaced by a healthy value system that is exclusively our own.

Burnout is total exhaustion operating on all of our subsystems — mental, emotional, physical and spiritual. It strips away our ability to make rational decisions. Many people feel that there are simple solutions that will automatically remedy burnout — taking a break from the job, changing careers or a single, drastic step such as divorce or separation. In reality, dealing with burnout requires a complete reevaluation of our priorities in life, as well as of our ability to accomplish those priorities rationally.

Since success in our society is equated primarily with the acquisition of material goods, we have been taught that the more you own, the more you are valued, and the more highly you should value yourself. Sadly, all too often this represents an unattainable ideal — competition, entrepreneurship, imagination and accomplishment taken to an unrealistic extreme. How many of us, in the process of blindly chasing this ideal, have consciously or unconsciously lost our peace of mind? Most likely, we have failed to achieve that vaguely defined, perfect lifestyle. So, why not replace the god of materialism with a renewed sense of purpose, supported with a practical and humane value system? We can learn to achieve worthwhile objectives without relentless greed and striving. Any rewards or material gains should be thought of as an accompanying benefit, *not* the primary objective of life.

Freeing the Prisoner Within

This book has described how burnout occurs, and its psychological, emotional and physical consequences. One of the main themes is that some people are able to cope quite effectively, while others must learn to do so.

It is certainly ironic that, while we live in what is popularly termed the "Information Age," on the personal level, our own thoughts and beliefs often constitute a closed system. We generally hear only what we want to hear, and will rigidly maintain a faulty belief system, even if it is causing us grief and pain.

Recognizing the automatic nature of the redundancy in our lives, both in the way we think and act, is a major step toward personal grow and balance. This understanding will maximize our sense of self-mastery and compassionate understanding, and relieve our pain and suffering.

Most of us fear change. We are held psychologically captive by a most demanding taskmaster — ourselves. Yet, unless we are willing to change, we will remain enslaved by our own fears, doubts and uncertainties. The main obstacle to overcome is that change itself represents uncertainty, and, usually, emotional *discomfort* — that ghastly emotion that we all barricade ourselves against.

No one relishes the idea, or even the experience, of change. But, to grow as individuals, we must accept that change is unavoidable and necessary. Contrary to the opinion of many contemporary "self-help" books, change is not easily initiated or accomplished. Rather, pain and uncertainty are all part of the process of change. The good news is that the pain of change *will* dissipate with the passage of time, as self-confidence and self-worth are nurtured and grow.

Change represents upheaval, losing something in order to gain something else, and acknowledging the failure of a previous concept or process. Change can be exciting when it is fully understood. Change for change's sake, of course, is counter-productive. Yet, when change comes about as the re-

Recognizing the automatic nature of the redundancy in our lives, both in the way we think and act, is a major step toward personal grow and balance. This understanding will maximize our sense of self-mastery and compassionate understanding, and relieve our pain and suffering.

sult of understanding, awareness and compassion, it produces exciting and positive experiences.

Personal transformation is *never* easy. Progress does not follow a straight line, nor is it accomplished quickly. However, by casting off long-held values and beliefs that are no longer congruent with the life we want for ourselves, we will attain our goals of change, growth and congruency with our environment.

A Life Process to Avoid Burnout

A thoroughly honest evaluation of who we are and how we relate to those around us creates a barrier against burnout.

Avoiding burnout is simple. We can begin by making a serious commitment to *understanding* ourselves and others better than we ever have before. This understanding does not involve judgments, nor does it require decisions. It is simply the objective of understanding the people and the circumstances that surround us. A thoroughly honest evaluation of who we are and how we relate to those around us creates a barrier against burnout.

If *understanding* is the first step in this process, *awareness* is the second. The ability to recognize, identify and assess a situation empowers each of us to remain in control of our lives. Such awareness allows us to enjoy our successes while keeping our setbacks in perspective.

Once we have developed understanding and awareness, we can move to a state of *compassion* that allows us to redirect our life toward a higher purpose. Moving outside of our own self-interest in the service of others links us into a broader network of compassion. Mahatma Gandhi spelled this out when he said, "God demands nothing less than complete self-surrender as the price for the only real freedom worth having. And when a person thus loses themselves, they immediately find themselves in the service of all that lives. It becomes their delight and recreation."

Deciding on one's preferred *direction* in life is also part of the process. Too many of us pigeon-hole ourselves into a single role in life, leaving no space for reevaluation. The wise child who is asked what he wants to be when he grows up, replies, "I really don't know. I'd like to be a kid first!" Here is someone who has already allowed room in his life for options and refuses to submit to outside pressures. We are not obligated to always know what we are going to do with the rest of our lives! Direction means creating opportunities for growth and change.

When we create a lifestyle in which our conscious and subconscious thought processes automatically reduce or eliminate excessive stress and anxiety, we have imbued our lives with *purpose.* Goals become achievable and long-lasting. The specter of burnout is neutralized. The age-old questions of, "Why are we here?" or "What is life all about?" no longer require an answer. The *process* of living our life becomes *what it is all about* — the journey is its own destination. Understanding our purpose in life becomes challenging, once it is fully understood that we must be most concerned with the *quality* of life.

The only obstacle to success in creating a healthy balance is a lack of discipline. We must take steps every day to maintain a harmony among our physical, emotional, mental and spiritual values.

Before we can share this success with others, we must recognize the energy demands associated with both positive and negative activity. To protect our inner lives, we must guard our outer lives as well. This requires an ongoing process of self-evaluation and questioning. We must ask ourselves:

- ○ How's my pace? Am I too busy?
- ○ Does my lifestyle allow me only enough time to race through a book or magazine, or does it also give me enough time to react to it?

We are not obligated to always know what we are going to do with the rest of our lives! Direction means creating opportunities for growth and change.

- Does my pace allow me to keep in touch with myself — with my inner needs, feelings and longings?
- Do I allow myself enough time to think, plan, make changes?
- Do I allow myself enough time to carefully observe and deal with the physical and emotional needs of those around me?
- Am I living, or just existing?

And, finally, if the answers to these questions suggest that things are not what they should be, we must have the courage to change — to gear down to a different tempo. Force of habit alone often keeps us on an anxious and stress-laden path, driving us forward hurriedly and thoughtlessly, like a smoker who knows that every cigarette reduces his life span by 14 minutes, but keeps reaching for another.

We only change our outer lives after our inner lives change, and that change begins with a *decision*. Shifting down to a simpler, less-harried existence is not easy. It requires a great deal of discipline and courage. The up side of slowing down is increased self-knowledge, self-compassion and compassion for others. We become a little less of an island unto ourselves in the midst of humanity, and our vision of ourselves as a part of a greater whole becomes clearer as we see that we are not alone in the world.

Always remember:

Use optimism as a beacon, and fully participate in the present with a clear vision of the future. The wisdom of the past will provide you with the courage to create new beginnings, desires, plans and dreams.

References

Chapter Two —
The Myth of the All-American Home

March of Dimes, Birth Defects Foundation. *Are You In a Safe Relationship? Prevention of Battering During Pregnancy.* Los Angeles: March of Dimes, Birth Defects Foundation, 1989.

Mehren, Elizabeth, & Herman Wong. "Psychological Warfare at Home." *Los Angeles Times* 20June1991.

National Center for Health Statistics. "Births, Marriages, Divorces, and Deaths." *Monthly Vital Statistics Report* 39.1(1990).

Chapter Three —
Who's Confused About Sex Roles?
Almost Everybody!

"APA Task Force Offers Facts, Ideas on Crisis of Women's Depression." *Brain Mind Bulletin* 14.12(1989): 3.

Astin, Alexander W., et al. *The American Freshman: National Norms for Fall 1988.* Los Angeles: The Cooperative Institutional Research Program, Higher Education Research Institute, University of California, Los Angeles, 1988.

Buscio, Michalene. "New Era in Battling Sexism." *Press-Telegram* 1August1991.

Centers for Disease Control. *Mortality and Morbidity Weekly Report* 21Sept1991.

Israeloff, Roberta. "Steady as She Goes: Balancing Work, Family, and Leisure." *Working Woman* July 1991: 79-81.

McGrath, Ellen, et al. *Women and Depression: Risk Factors and Treatment Issues.* Washington: American Psychological Association, 1990.

Merton, Andrew. "Father Hunger: A New Generation of Men Struggling to Become the Fathers They Never Had." *New Age Journal* Sep/Oct 1986: 22-72.

Time. Special Issue: "Women: The Road Ahead." (Fall 1990).

Chapter Four —
The Human Arson in Our Schools

Business Week. *Endangered Species: Children of Promise.*

Eng, Lily. "School Cuts Affecting Cherished Programs." *Los Angeles Times*: A1

"Majority of 2,000 Oregon Residents Fail Literacy Survey." Associated Press item, April 1991.

Richter, Paul. "Survival of the Fittest Schools." *Los Angeles Times* 18May1991.

Teacher magazine. Oct 1989 and Jan 1991 issues.

Chapter Five —
Fear and Loathing in the American Workplace

Briggs, David. "Bishops Report Many Priests Suffering From Burnout." *Press Democrat*, 26December1988: A10.

California Department of Industrial Relations, Division of Labor Statistics and Research. *California Work Injuries And Illness.* San Francisco: Division of Labor Statistics and Research, 1987.

California Workers' Compensation Institute. *Research Notes, Mental Stress Claims In California Workers' Compensation: Incidence, Costs and Trends.* San Francisco: June 1990.

Carter, David L., and Darrel W. Stephens. *Drug Abuse By Police Officers: An Analysis of Critical Policy Issues.* Springfield, Illinois: Charles C. Thomas, Publisher, 1988, 5.

Cherniss, C. Staff Burnout. *Job Stress and the Human Services.* Beverly Hills: Sage, 1980.

County Supervisors Association of California. *Stress Related Disability Retirements, A Special Report Prepared for the Assembly Public Employees, Retirement And Social Security Committee.* Sacramento: County Supervisors Association of California, 1987.

Fishkin, Gerald Loren. *Firefighter and Paramedic Burnout — The Survival Guide: The Role You Play.* Los Angeles: HBJ, 1989.

Fishkin, Gerald Loren. *Police Burnout — Signs, Symptoms and Solutions.* Los Angeles: Legal and Professional Publications-HBJ, 1988.

Freudenberger, H. J. "Staff Burnout." *Journal of Social Issues,* 30 (1974): 159-165.

Freudenberger, H. J. "The staff burnout syndrome in alternative institutions." *Psychotherapy: Theory, Research, and Practice,* 12 (1975): 73-82.

Levy, Barry, "Occupational Health in the United States: Its Relevance to the Health Professional," *Occupational Health,* ed. Barry Levy and D. Wegman. (Boston: Little Brown, 1983).

McGraw, Carol. "Employers, Workers Act to Fight Job Harassment." *Los Angeles Times* 21Oct1990.

Schroepfer, Lisa. "The Men's Health Job Stress Index." *Men's Health.* Aug 1991.

Shore, Glen M. "Occupational Disease Compensation In California." California Policy Seminar, Research Report, University of California at Berkeley, 1987.

"Stress at Work: How Can We Cope?" *Newsweek On Health* Summer 1988: 34-35.

United States. Department of Occupational Health and Safety. *1986 Annual Death and Injury Survey.* Washington: GPO, 1986.

Chapter Six —
Retirement — Making a Positive Transition

Rosenblatt, Robert A. "Bankruptcy as Part of Medicare Feared." *Los Angeles Times* 18May1991: A21.

Schwadel, Francine. "Turning Conservative, Baby Boomers Reduce Their Frivolous Buying." *Wall Street Journal* 19June1991: A1+.

Chapter Seven —
The Human Burnout Syndrome — When and How It Began

Cunningham, George. "Boredom and Burnout." *Press Telegram*, 20Aug1990.

National Center for Health Statistics. "Advance Report of Final Mortality Statistics, 1987." *Monthly Vital Statistics Report*, Vol 38, No. 5. Hyattsville, Maryland: Public Health Service. 1989.

O'Malley, Michael. *Keeping Watch: A History of American Time.* New York: Viking-Penguin, 1990.

Szanton, Eleanor. Executive Director, National Center for Clinical Infant Programs. Personal interview. 29May1990.

Chapter Eight —
Stress, Anxiety and Depression — The Early Stages of Burnout

Beck, Joan. "Depression: It's Not Just the 'Blues'." *Press Telegram* 23Oct1990: B5.

Bower, Bruce. "A Melancholy Breach: Science and Clinical Tradition Clash Amid New Insights Into Depression." *Science News* 26Jan1991.

"Chronic Fatigue Syndrome." *Newsweek* 12Nov1990.

Gold, Deborah, et al. "Chronic Fatigue: A Prospective and Virologic Study." *Journal of the American Medical Association.* July 1990: 48-53.

Hymowitz, Carol. "Stepping Off the Fast Track." *Wall Street Journal* 13 June 1989: B1.

National Council on Alcoholism, Inc. *Business, Industry And Time In A Bottle.* Los Angeles: Los Angeles County Office On Alcohol Abuse & Alcoholism.

"Occupational Alcoholism Programs thru Union Contracts." Washington: International Association of Machinists and Aerospace Workers.

Roan, Shari. "When Stress Keeps You up Nights." *Los Angeles Times* 2Apr1991: E1+.

Selye, Hans. *The Stress of Life.* New York: McGraw-Hill, 1956.

Selye, Hans. *Stress Without Distress.* New York: Harper & Row, 1974.

Selye, Hans. *The Physiology and Pathology of Exposure to Stress.* Montreal: ACTA, 1950.

Selye, Hans. "On Stress Without Distress," *Executive Health* 11.11 (1975).

Selye, Hans. "On Stress and the Executive," *Executive Health* 9.4 (1978).

Wells, Kenneth B., et al. "Detection of Depressive Disorder for Patients Receiving Prepaid or Fee-for-Service Care: Results From the Medical Outcome Study." *Journal of the American Medical Association.* December 1989.

Chapter Nine —
Working Through a Life Crisis

American Psychiatric Association. *Diagnostic and Statistical Manual of Mental Disorders.* 3rd ed. Washington: APA, 1987.

Ebersole, P., and Joan Flores. "Positive Impact of Life Crisis." *Journal of Social Behavior and Personality* 4.5 (1989): 463-469.

McClinton, James L. "The Lessons of Hurricane Hugo: Expecting the Unexpected." *The Police Chief* Sep 1990.

Chapter Ten —
Burnout — A Modern American Epidemic

Charles, Sara C., and Eugene Kennedy. *Defendant, A Psychiatrist on Trial for Medical Malpractice.* New York: Vintage Books, 1985.

Garden, Anna-Maria. "Burnout: The effect of psychological type on research findings." *Journal of Occupational Psychology.* Sep 1989: 223-234.

Giges, Nancy. "Burnout." *Advertising Age* 10Apr1989: A1+.

Chapter Eleven —
Solutions for Dealing with Burnout

Frankl, Viktor E. *Man's Search For Meaning.* New York: Simon and Schuster, 1962.

Jacobson, Edmund. *You Must Relax.* New York: McGraw Hill, 1978.

Index

A

absenteeism 25, 32, 45, 85-86, 94, 119, 123
abuse 15, 20, 22, 24-26, 41, 65, 68, 85, 87, 89, 90, 121, 123
adrenaline 69-70, 75-76, 82, 93, 139
aggression 9, 109
alarm 69-70, 83, 92
American Dream 1, 5, 111
anger 71, 74, 76, 83-84, 87-88, 91, 101, 103, 107
anxiety 100-102, 108
apprehension 75, 93
assertion training 91, 143, 147
attitudes 105
automatic mode 3
autonomic nervous system 74, 93

B

Baby Boomers 17, 51, 54
balance 10-11, 27-29, 33, 67-68, 70, 84, 92, 102, 104, 115, 120, 127, 130, 132, 134-135, 140
battle fatigue 101
bingeing 77, 94
bipolar thinking 83
blame 2-5, 38, 65, 66, 87, 121, 126, 129
boundary problems 122
breathing exercises 140, 147
burnout 1-5, 8, 33, 38, 42, 47, 61-62, 66-68, 70, 74, 76, 84-85, 92, 98, 102, 111-115, 117-123, 125, 127-130, 133, 138-139, 142-143, 146
    coping with 14, 102

C

catharsis 131, 146
change 129-130, 133-135, 143-144
chemical dependency 89
child abuse 20, 22
chronic fatigue syndrome 80-81, 94, 161
clergy 41-43, 47
closure 36, 114, 122, 131, 146
co-dependent 87-88, 95
cognitive restructuring 103, 109, 131, 146
communication 13, 37, 44, 57, 62-64, 66, 76, 92-93, 131, 136, 146
compassion 90, 104-105
compulsive dependency 65-66
compulsive disorders 65-66, 77, 94, 132
crisis 3, 20, 23, 34-35, 55, 80, 83, 97, 98, 100, 101-105, 108-109, 126, 143-144, 147
    intervention 35, 102, 104, 109, 144, 147

D

death 16, 22, 40, 50, 55, 70, 82, 84, 98-100, 106, 108, 115, 118, 120
defense mechanisms 69, 70, 76, 143, 147
denial 2, 4, 9, 11, 64-66, 76, 88-89, 95, 108, 135, 143
depletion 80
depression 14-15, 20-21, 41, 43, 56, 69-71, 80-87, 94, 100-102, 115, 117, 122, 127, 130-132, 135, 137, 144, 145
despair 4, 20, 80, 84-85, 92, 98, 103-104, 109, 115, 118, 130, 136
detoxification 41, 89, 90, 95

About the Author

GERALD LOREN FISHKIN, PH.D., AUTHOR, lecturer and psychotherapist, is an internationally recognized authority on stress and burnout. Dr. Fishkin holds a doctorate in Clinical Psychology. His theories are based not only on scientific fact and current research, but on his 23 years of experience as a treating clinician.

He is a corporate and governmental consultant on worker stress and burnout. Currently, he is the consulting Behavioral Science editor for the *American Fire Journal.*

As an expert in clinical and forensic hypnosis, Dr. Fishkin also works with victims and witnesses of violent crimes in scene reconstruction and suspect identification.

The concept of burnout Dr. Fishkin has developed is an extension of the late Dr. Hans Selye's General Adaptation Syndrome. In essence, Dr. Fishkin shows that, when we are repeatedly exposed to a stressor, our natural response is to accommodate and deal with it using whatever coping skills we may have developed over the years. Unfortunately, these coping mechanisms may be maladaptive, leading to destructive behaviors such as alcoholism; compulsive eating, spending or sexual behavior; hostility; or emotional withdrawal. Left untreated, burnout can lead to depression, physical illness or even death.

Dr. Fishkin's previous books are *Police Burnout — Signs, Symptoms and Solutions* (1988), and *Firefighter and Paramedic Burnout — The Survival Guide: The Role You Play* (1989), published by Harcourt Brace Jovanovich, Legal and Professional Publications, Inc.

Dr. Fishkin has appeared on over 100 television and radio programs nationally, and was a featured guest on both the Geraldo Rivera show and Michael Jackson's syndicated radio talk show. He has been published extensively in national and international magazines and newspapers, writing on a variety of issues related to stress and burnout. His biography has appeared in *Who's Who in the West* since 1978.

Dr. Fishkin lives in the South Bay area of Los Angeles with his wife Kathy and two unconditionally loving Lhasa Apsos.

ORDERING INFORMATION

If your local book seller is out of
American Dream, American Burnout —
How to Cope When it All Gets to Be Too Much,
you may order additional copies by phone or mail.

Price: **$16.95**
shipping and handling:
$3.50 for first book
$1.25 each additional book

CA orders please add 8.25% sales tax ($1.23 per book)
MI orders please add 4% sales tax (68¢ per book)

TELEPHONE ORDERS

Toll Free
1-800-345-0096
8 a.m. to 8 p.m. (Eastern), M-F
Visa and MasterCard accepted

(in Michigan and outside the U.S.)
(616) 276-5196

FAX ORDERS
(616) 276-5197

MAIL ORDERS
Send check or money order to:

Publishers Distribution Service
6893 Sullivan Road
Grawn, MI 49637

Quantity discounts available